# NEW SONG
## in the
# ANDES

# NEW SONG
## in the
# ANDES

## JOHN MAUST

**WILLIAM CAREY LIBRARY**
**Pasadena, California**

Published by
WILLIAM CAREY LIBRARY
P.O. Box 40129
Pasadena, California 91114
(818) 798-0819
    In cooperation with
GOSPEL MISSIONARY UNION
10000 North Oak
Kansas City, Missouri 64155
    Canadian office:
2121 Henderson Hwy.
Winnipeg, MB R2G 1P8

---

Library of Congress Cataloging-in-Publication Data

Maust, John
    New song in the Andes / John Maust
        p.    cm.
    Bibliography: p.
    ISBN 0-87808-219-0
    1. Quechua Indians—Missions. 2. Missions—Ecuador—
Chimborazo—History. 3. Gospel Missionary Union. 4. Missionaries—
Ecuador—Chimborazo—Biography. 5. Chimborazo (Ecuador)—
Biography.
    I. Title.
F2230.2.K4M378 1989
266'.0089983—dc20                                    89-35170
                                                          CIP

---

Text Design by Jone M. Bosch and Dave Shaver

# CONTENTS

# Foreword

Like a bomb waiting to go off, the Chimborazo story had to be told. It is surely the most outstanding case of a dramatic missionary breakthrough to the Indians of the Americas, on a large scale, in modern times. It is so significant that the very word, Chimborazo, sends shivers up my spine. In light of the 500th anniversary of Columbus "discovering" America, let's stand back and look at the Chimborazo event in its crucial context.

1. A generalization would have to be that Europeans arriving in the "new world" have mainly simply killed off the native Americans in North America, Central America and South America.

2. A number of outstanding missionary breakthroughs have been destroyed by other, non-missionary Europeans who had quite different goals.

3. Those native Americans that did not die from our European diseases, forced labor, or direct warfare, have been pervasively resistant to both our Gospel and our European ways. Being a missionary to Spanish or Portuguese-speakers in Latin America involves one-tenth the complexity of making sense in the exotic Indians languages of Latin America. No, not one-tenth. One-hundredth.

4. The largest single remaining community of native Americans are the survivors of the Inca empire in the high Andes running 3,000 miles from Ecuador in the north to Bolivia in the south, well over 10 million who speak various dialects of Quichua/Quechua. This includes Chimborazo.

OK, so how in the world did the Gospel break through, massively at Chimborazo? Well, truth is stranger than fiction. What a fascinating story. What pregnant meaning for perhpas the whole of the Andes range. And what a marvelous thing it is to have this incredible story so beautifully and skillfully told! John, we are all indebted to you, deeply.

Ralph D. Winter
September 1991
Pasadena, California

# Preface

I have special memories of 1979, year of my first trip to Latin America. The midnight flight from Chicago had arrived in Quito, Ecuador, about 5 a.m. And within a couple of hours, missionary Henry Klassen had loaded me into his Land Rover for the four-hour drive to mountainous Chimborazo Province.

With the windows jiggling, tape recorder rolling and my head nodding from lack of sleep, Klassen began telling about an amazing spiritual breakthrough among the Quichuas in Ecuador's Chimborazo Province. Quichuas? I knew next to nothing about them and could barely even pronounce their name.

But in the next few days, I witnessed the unique vitality of the fast-growing Quichua church. Literally, an entire people and their way of life had been transformed by Christ.

The way that Klassen and other missionaries and Quichua church leaders described it, this was a story that needed to be told. Five subsequent trips to the region over the next nine years confirmed to me that this was true.

The book in your hands is the fruit of those trips, interviews and investigation. I pray that it does justice to God's work among this dear people in the Ecuadorian Andes.

Special thanks go to Henry and Pat Klassen, Roberta Hostetter, Mary Warkentine, Phyllis Blum and other GMU missionaries for their hospitality during my stays at the Colta mission station.

I would also like to thank the late James L. Johnson, author and Wheaton Graduate School professor who encouraged me to write the Quichua story, even though Christian publishers said "mission books don't sell."

Thanks must also go to the late Manual Naula Sagñay, the first Quichua medical doctor, who invited me to conduct a Christian writers workshop among the Quichuas in

ix

1982. He died tragically of cancer at the age of 44 in January 1985.

I also think of Dr. Ralph Winter, missions expert at the U.S. Center for World Mission in Pasadena, California. Each time I bumped into Winter, he said, "Where's that book about the Quichuas? Well, if nobody else will publish it, we will, for crying out loud."

My mother, Roseanna Maust, also deserves a special word of appreciation. She and other prayer warriors at the Nappanee, Indiana, First Brethren Church kept praying this book would be finished and published even when I had about given up hope.

I also want to thank Media Director Abe Reddekopp of Gospel Missionary Union, for his patience and support through the long writing and editing process, and also John Rasmussen of Latin America Mission, who gave me the time and freedom to pursue this writing project apart from other duties at LAM.

Let me preface the following narrative with a few comments. First, this book occasionally describes Roman Catholic opposition in Chimborazo through the eyes of evangelicals who experienced it, but there is absolutely no intent of "attacking" Roman Catholics or placing their leaders in an unfavorable light. Indeed, we can rejoice that Roman Catholic/Protestant relations in Ecuador have eased since the beginning of the Quichua work.

This book focuses specifically on the Quichua church in Ecuador's Chimborazo Province, but that is not to shortchange church growth among Quichuas in other parts of Ecuador. And I especially focus on the work of Gospel Missionary Union—not because it has done a "better" job in Ecuador than other evangelical agencies, but because GMU pioneered and developed the Quichua work in Chimborazo and because it remains the primary agency working among them.

To give continuity to the book, I have described the Quichua story mostly through the eyes and experiences of two Gospel Missionary Union workers—Julia Anderson Woodward and Henry Klassen.

Woodward pioneered the outreach and stuck with it for half a century. In the early chapters of this book, most of Mrs. Woodward's words and experiences come directly from her letters and articles from GMU's magazine, *The Gospel Message*, and from interviews with former missionary associates. Klassen went to Ecuador the year Woodward retired, 1953. He witnessed and participated in the entire Quichua church growth story—from the first Quichua baptism in 1954 to the initial breakthroughs and subsequent widespread conversions.

Again, this is not to ignore the many other GMU missionaries who faithfully worked or still work among the Chimborazo Quichuas. Some are named in this book, and all will be rewarded by our Lord for their faithful service.

Sometimes this book refers to Quichuas as "Indians," an inaccurate term but the one most often used years ago. It should be noted that Quichuas today prefer to be called an "indigenous group," not Indians, and in their own language they go by *Runa*, meaning "human being."

I conducted hours of in-depth interviews with Quichua church leaders. Characteristically reticent to discuss their past, they nevertheless were very open and generous with me. Their input proved invaluable to this story. And of course the real story of the Quichua church will have to be written by a qualified Quichua. What a story that will be!

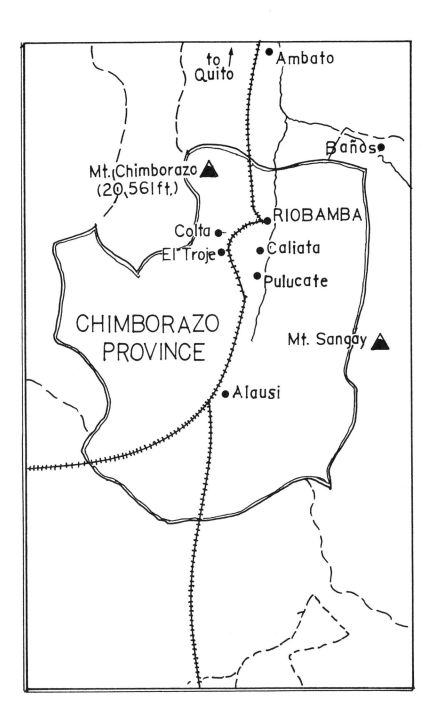

# WOMEN FIRST

"Julia, they've chosen us!"

Ella Ozman said it so breathlessly, fellow missionary Julia Anderson had to laugh.

"What have they chosen us for?" Julia teased.

"The mission has decided that you and I be the ones to go to the Quichuas."

Julia's smile began to fade as her friend continued. "Isn't it exciting?" Thinking perhaps that sounded too frivolous, Ella added, "I mean, isn't it a wonderful responsibility that's being entrusted to us?"

Julia nodded mechanically. She did not know what to say or even think. Would the mission really send them—two single women still in their early twenties—into an unevangelized area of Ecuador that was inhabited by Indians and without a single Protestant missionary?

The year was 1902 and missionaries of Gospel Missionary Union were gathered for a spiritual retreat in Ambato, Ecuador. Julia had arrived in Ecuador only about four years previously in November 1898. Based in the coastal city of Guayaquil, Julia had just begun to master the language and contribute to the Spanish work. Surely the mission would not send her into a totally new ministry now. As for Ella, she was new on the field and did not even speak Spanish, much less Quichua.

But Julia knew that when mission director George Fisher made a decision about something, he rarely changed his mind. Fisher was the son of missionaries to Jamaica. As a young man, he became secretary of the Young Men's Christian Associations for the state of Kansas. After several years under Fisher's tireless leadership, the state's YMCA chapters and church-joining converts doubled in number.

At a state YMCA meeting in 1889, Fisher's passion for souls caught fire and blazed outside Kansas to the entire world. Conference speakers had graphically depicted the world's spiritual need, singling out the Sudan—a land 4,000 miles long and 1,000 miles wide, a land of sixty million souls without Christ or a missionary to take him there. And one morning, several young men offered themselves as missionaries to the African nation.

Later that day one of the potential missionaries, Will Mitchell, went boating with a friend. In animated conversation about the needs of the heathen, they forgot to watch where they were going. The current swept them over a small dam, and Mitchell drowned.

Emotion gripped the packed assembly hall as men carried inside the lifeless body of the would-be missionary.

"God has spoken to us this day!" rasped conference speaker James H. Brookes in an unforgettable address.

And for George Fisher, this was God's message: Every believer was needed in the urgent campaign of world evangelization. For every Will Mitchell who fell, countless others must step forward to take his or her place.

Fisher threw himself into the promotion of foreign missions among Kansas YMCA chapters. The missions emphasis quickly spread to YMCAs and Christian groups in other states, so that in 1892 Fisher and men and women of like mind formed the World's Gospel Union (renamed Gospel Missionary Union in 1901).

The new mission sent its very first missionaries to Morocco in 1894. Then at an all-night prayer meeting during a Nebraska Bible conference the following year, a spiritual burden for Ecuador feel over the entire group. They named

Fisher and two others to go to Ecuador even though Protestant missionaries were still forbidden there.

In faith, Fisher went to the Ecuadorian consulate in Washington, D.C., to apply for visas. The official told him a revolution had just taken place, and that the new liberal government under General Eloy Alfaro would allow foreign Protestant missionaries to enter Ecuador and also see they would be protected. The amazed Fisher could only praise God.

About a year later, in 1896, Fisher, J. A. Strain and F. W. Farnol disembarked in Guayaquil. A US consulate official advised them to keep on going to Peru, less fanatical and so less risky for Protestant workers than staunchly Catholic Ecuador. But the missionaries were not about to go home now.

The three missionaries even arranged an interview with Ecuador's new President Alfaro, who happened to be in Guayaquil at the time. The general seemed pleased when Fisher said the United States was very interested in the cause of freedom in Ecuador.

Most of the priests had left the coastal area when his liberal forces moved in, Alfaro said. He could offer the Protestant missionaries his protection on the coast. But for the time being, he could not guarantee their safety in the interior.

### Burden for the Quichuas

Now, in 1902, the GMU workers were meeting in the interior, in the Andes mountain city of Ambato. George Fisher had observed the hundreds of Quichuas milling about the city's open-air markets and felt a spiritual burden for them.

"These people need Jesus Christ," he exclaimed to the missionaries. "Descendants of the Incas," he called them.

Ironically, Ambato was the hometown of Ecuador's foremost literary figure, Juan Montalvo, who had died about thirteen years earlier. It was Montalvo who penned that infamous description of Ecuador's Indians.

3

"If my pen had the gifts of tears," he wrote, "I would write a book entitled the Indian and make the world weep."

The Quichuas had groveled in virtual slavery to the Spanish landlords ever since the Spanish conquest. The Spaniards kept the Indians at the bottom rung on the social ladder, and landlords treated them like property and sometimes worse than farm animals. The Spanish were not able to erase the Quichuas' language and customs, but they did take something more precious: the Quichuas' self-respect.

Whereas Montalvo rightly lamented the Quichuas' physical and social suffering, Fisher looked particularly to the Indians' spiritual bondage. In his view, the Spanish culture had imposed a loveless version of Roman Catholicism that did little or nothing to inspire personal liberating faith in Jesus Christ.

The Quichuas' religion mainly consisted of drunken feasts in honor of the saints, Fisher believed. They needed to hear the gospel. The Quichuas' poverty and physical suffering were bad, but what could be worse than eternity in hell?

Fisher challenged his missionary cohorts on this point, and he asked them to pray about missionary outreach to the Quichuas. Before the Ambato conference ended, the assembled body proposed that two single women move quietly into some Quichua settlement and win the people's confidence.

The task would not be easy. Their witness would inspire opposition, if not persecution, from the religious and political authorities. Several years earlier, a customs official in Guayaquil had tried to refuse a shipment of Bibles and hymnals, saying, "As long as Mt. Chimborazo stands, these books will never enter Ecuador." It would take a real miracle to reach the Quichuas for Christ.

## Going to Chimborazo

The rumors were true. Julia Anderson and Ella Ozman were asked to report to Fisher. Unusually tall for her day—nearly six feet—Julia never slouched as more self-conscious women might have done. And so the tall blond Shelton, Iowa, native became an immediate focus of attention for Ecuadorian don Juans. Julia quickly learned to close her ears to their whistles and catcalls.

"Julia, Ella, please come in," Fisher said. He firmly shook each woman's hand. Then he showed them to their seats and strode to a chair of his own. Fisher seemed to breathe purpose.

"Well, what did you think of the missionary conference?" he asked, not allowing time for an awkward silence.

"I found it very inspiring," Ella said.

"Yes, very challenging," Julia added.

"I'm glad you thought so," Fisher said. "Besides being a time of Christian fellowship, these meetings provide a time of seeking God's direction.

"You probably know why I've called you here," Fisher said to Julia and Ella. "The mission feels strongly that we must take the gospel to the Quichua Indians."

Pausing for a moment, he continued, "And we think it best to send women missionaries. They will be less threatening to the Indians than men."

Ella and Julia traded glances, as Fisher got to the point.

"You have been chosen to go there. We would like for you to move in among the Indians and start learning the language…to go to this people where Christ is not named."

"I would consider it a privilege to serve among the Quichuas," said Ella before Julia could collect her thoughts.

"Praise the Lord," said Fisher. "And you, Julia? You look a little unsure."

"Well, I certainly desire the Lord's will. I hope I am capable of such a task."

"I'm sure you are," said Fisher. "Will Reed has spoken very highly of you. He said you have developed into an effective witness during your short time in Ecuador."

Reed, another of the GMU missionaries in Ecuador, had been Julia's pastor back in Iowa, where he had opened a training school for missionaries and Christian workers in the town of Avoca. It was Reed who planted Julia's desire

5

to become a missionary. He had gone to Ecuador in 1896, and Julia went there herself two years later.

The meeting with Fisher quickly ended. The director said they would be going to Chimborazo Province, home for an estimated 150,000 Quichuas. There had really been no question whether they would go. But afterwards Julia confessed her doubts to her former pastor Will Reed.

"I wonder if I'm the one to go—if I'm really qualified," she said.

"You'll do fine," Reed assured her, appreciative of Julia's transparency. She was not like some missionaries, who tried to hide their doubts or weaknesses.

"Just don't take yourself too seriously," he said. "God will use you."

"You know," she said, smiling at herself. "I hate the idea of giving up my nice room with the Chapman family in Guayaquil."

"Well, you'll have to work that one out with the Lord," said Reed, chuckling.

Departure day arrived, and Julia packed only a few items: some clothes and woolen underwear for the mountain cold, a favorite book of poetry, a Spanish Bible and her well-worn English one and writing materials for her diary and language study.

What she desired most was a big supply of God's care and direction. She remembered her life verse, Romans 10:11: "Whosoever believeth on him shall not be ashamed."

She left her Guayaquil home, taking one last glance at her clean room with its shiny board floor and white wallpaper. It would be a long time before she had a place like that again.

# 2

# QUICHUA COUNTRY

Julia felt almost seasick as her horse swayed back and forth up the mountain trail. The dirt path clung to the sides of the mountains, while seemingly bottomless ravines dropped off below.

"Hold on tight!" she called to Ella.

"I most certainly am!" Ella's legs squeezed her horse's flanks as a drowning man would his life preserver.

Jerome Altig, a fellow missionary, had volunteered to accompany the women to their destination. And when the missionaries reached Riobamba, the capital of Chimborazo Province, they were met by an employee of the the hacienda owner on whose property Julia and Ella would be living. Another four hours' travel by horseback awaited them.

Julia and Ella eyed each other as their guide motioned for them to follow. The horses quickly headed south and uphill from Riobamba.

Each bend in the trail boasted a spectacular new sight. Tiny multi-colored plots of barley and potatoes covered the bald slopes like checkerboards. This was Ecuador's Central Valley, a narrow 250-mile-long plateau bordered by mountain ranges. Ella and Julia were already feeling the effects of the two-mile-high altitude. Several snow-capped peaks towered even higher above them—some of the thirty or so extinct or active volcanoes lining the plateau's bordering rims.

Most prominent was majestic Chimborazo at 20,561 feet above sea level. It stood like a silent sentinel some forty miles to the north of their future home. Sometimes clouds covered its peak; other times its snowy crown stood out in colorful glory.

Centuries before, the Puruhá tribe had fashioned their intricate weavings in the shadow of Chimborazo. Then near the end of the fifteenth century, Tupa Inca mobilized an army of 200,000 Inca warriors, who easily crushed the Puruhás in a relentless march north from present-day Peru.

As they did to all conquered tribes, the Incas imposed their Quechua language on the indigenous groups in southern Ecuador. Over time the dialect in this region became known as Quichua (KEE-CHOO-WAH), not Quechua as in present-day Peru and Bolivia, because it basically operated without the "e" and "o" vowel sounds. The people became known as Quichuas.

Rampaging Spanish armies arrived in Ecuador only a few decades after the Inca conquest. So since the 1530s, the Quichuas and other tribal groups had lived in submission to the Spanish authorities and culture.

As their horses continued south from Riobamba, the missionaries eyed a lower peak, Tulubú, standing by itself in a valley to the east. Its top was flat, rather than cone-shaped. According to Quichua legend, Tulubú had wanted to become king of the mountains and challenged Chimborazo to a fight. Chimborazo stepped on him and flattened him out.

Farther ahead, the missionaries spotted a jagged peak puffing smoke: Sangay. It was an active volcano, one of three in the area. Sometimes Sangay would rumble for a week without stopping.

Again, the Quichuas had an explanation. "That's where sinners go to hell," some said. "When it shoots its top, that means the devils are clamoring for another soul."

Small adobe houses spotted the hillsides, and silo-shaped stacks of barley stood alongside. The fibrous thorn-edged

8

century plants, which Quichuas used to make rope, grew everywhere.

Quichuas closely watched the women as they rode by, and Julia and Ella felt uncomfortable until they realized they were staring back just as much.

Facially, the Quichuas resembled the bronze-skinned Indians the women had seen in the United States. The Quichua woman wore straight ankle-length woolen garments, fastened at the waist by a rainbow-colored woven belt. A pin fastened her woolen cape at the throat, and bright beaded necklaces and bracelets completed her attire.

The Quichua man wore white muslin trousers reaching just below the knee, plus a poncho covering a wool shirt. Both men and women wore hats—the most common having a white oval crown and a flat brim. The woman's hair fell in coal-black locks to either side of her face and from behind in a long braid wrapped in a narrow strip of brightly-colored cloth.

Everyone—men, women and children—went barefoot. How could they bear the cold and rocky trails without shoes? the missionaries wondered.

## Touch of something familiar

Prior arrangements had been made with an English-speaking farmer, who had offered the missionaries a place to live on his farm. However, the farm's overseer had an extra house on his property in nearby Caliata, so he took them there. Ella was elated by this change. Rather than living with an English-speaking farmer, they would immediately live among the Quichuas.

"Here we are!" the man announced, reining his horse into a muddy yard.

"This is our home?" Julia asked, looking skeptically at the one-room hut. There were no windows in the adobe walls, and Julia wondered if the thatched roof leaked.

The new surroundings fascinated but, at the same time, frightened Julia. It was one thing to leave Iowa farm country and adjust to the Spanish culture on the coast in Guayaquil. But this was something else entirely.

"Oh, for a touch of something familiar," she said half to herself, half to God.

Just then a small woman scurried from the side of the house, which she would share with them.

"You women must be very tired from your long trip," she said.

"This is Mamita Cruz," the overseer said. "She lives in the room attached to your house."

Anxious to welcome her new neighbors, the elderly woman began talking so fast in Spanish that Julia could barely understand her. The group dismounted, and Mamita fastidiously brushed mud and dust from the women's dresses. Mamita reminded Julia of dear grandmothers back home, and the missionary could not help but like her.

Just then a scrawny cat sauntered up and rubbed its head against Julia's ankle. Julia loved cats. And this one made the rounds to all the visitors. In the process, Mamita tripped over it. And seeing the tiny woman dance over the cat made Ella laugh. Mamita opened a wide, toothless grin.

"That cat!" she exclaimed. Grabbing Ella's arm, she said, "Let's go inside for a *cafecito*."

"What did she say?" Ella asked doubtfully, wishing she understood Spanish.

"She's inviting us inside for coffee," Julia interpreted.

"Oh, in that case, let's go," Ella said. This time, she tugged Mamita's arm, delighting the old woman, and they headed toward the door.

Between the grandma and her cat, Julia thought, "Maybe I'll feel at home after all." She ducked to go inside since the doorsill was only about four feet high.

The women had not brought any furniture. Inside was only a short bed, a small table, a bench and a wooden box. That night the missionaries were too tired to arrange their limited furnishings.

But Julia did manage to accommodate her long legs by extending her side of the bed with a washboard. At 13,000 feet above sea level, the two missionaries did not mind having to share a bed. Any extra warmth would be appreciated.

10

Before going to sleep, Julia wrote an entry in her diary for January 24, 1902—their first day in Quichua country. Surely God would bless this venture. There was no reason to expect otherwise.

# NEW IN TOWN

Icy fingers touched Julia's shoulder. "Ohhh," she gasped, abruptly awake.

"I'm sorry. I didn't mean to scare you," said Ella, giggling nervously. "I wanted you to listen to something."

Outside, something shuffled on the bare earth. It sounded like feet, then high-pitched whispers.

"I'll find out who, or what, it is," Julia said finally. Who would be visiting them at that hour? She stumbled out of her warm bed and started fumbling for her clothes in the dark unfamiliar room.

"No, we'll both find out," Ella said. She also got up, and the women nearly knocked each other over, groping for the door.

Julia finally threw it open. When she did, the rising sun momentarily blinded her. As her eyes focused, several short squat forms materialized into Quichua women. Julia asked them what they wanted. But no one seemed to understand Spanish.

"What should we do?" Ella whispered over her companion's shoulder.

Mamita Cruz answered that question for them. The gregarious neighbor emerged from her side of the house and placed herself between the Quichuas and the missionaries.

"You have your first visitors, eh, Señoritas?" Mamita said, then turned toward the Quichuas and spoke to them in their language. A spirited conversation quickly ensued.

"They say they've never seen yellow hair like yours," Mamita said, turning to Julia.

The missionary brushed at her mussed hair and tried not to appear self-conscious. ""But don't they want something?" she asked, changing the subject. The Quichua women tittered, covering their mouths with their ponchos.

"No. They just came to see you foreign ladies," said Mamita. "And they want to know if you have any medicines," Mamita said.

Medicines? The missionaries had not expected that request.

"Go and see what we have, while I stay out here with our new friends," Julia told Ella.

In a few minutes, Ella came back with a small armful of sacks and bottles. The Quichua visitors, who until then had stayed somewhat distant, crowded close to eye the provisions.

"Don't worry," Mamita said. "They'll pay you for it."

Julia and Ella tried to be fair in doling out small quantities of salts and quinine, peppermint tea and soda—the nearest things to medical supplies on hand. By now, the group had grown considerably and there was barely enough to go around.

Later the same day, just as Mamita said, the women did pay. Some brought barley, wheat or boiled potatoes. One woman sent her son with water he had fetched, and this pleased Julia and Ella, since the well was several hundred yards down the mountain.

During the next few days, the missionaries met most of their neighbors. For conversations with Quichuas who did not also speak Spanish, Mamita Cruz proudly served as interpreter.

From their hut, resting at the highest point in the village, the missionaries saw what looked like hundreds of Quichua homes. Someone told them 13,000 Quichuas lived in the immediate vicinity.

13

## Learning the language

Learning Quichua became Julia's abiding goal. She and Ella spent hours every day among the Quichuas—going to the potato patches, threshing floors or wherever people were found. Sometimes they carded wool with the Quichua women, and found themselves willing to do almost anything if it would help them learn the language.

The women took exhausting tramps on the mountain trails. Often they visited Quichua homes. The thatched roofs were usually charred black around the edges from the smoke from cooking fires inside. When they entered the huts, the missionaries quickly learned to stoop low beneath the rising smoke and then converse either on their haunches or sitting down.

When people understood Spanish, Julia read from her Bible and shared her testimony. Where people only spoke Quichua, Julia tried to learn new words and present herself as a friend.

The Quichua children made especially good language helpers. As the children tended their sheep and pigs on the mountainsides, Julia and Ella sat alongside. Julia often crocheted or knitted—all the while eavesdropping on conversations.

Sometimes the children looked ready to bolt at the sight of tall white women. But their fears melted under the strangers' warm smiles and gifts of candy. From the start, Julia planned to open a school in her home, where Quichua children could learn to read and write and study the Bible.

Every day became a new adventure. From observing the Quichuas, the missionaries learned to cook "Indian-style." Their stove consisted of a kettle resting on two large stones. They fed the fire with straw or wood. Because it took so long to cook potatoes, they sometimes cooked enough food to last three days.

Machca—the toasted barley flour that Quichuas ate for lunch in the fields—became one of the missionaries' favorites. Julia and Ella first toasted the grain and then ground it between stones. Mixed with sugar, the powdery substance made a tasty energy snack.

The missionaries also made their Indian hut more liveable. They had their walls whitewashed and a window put in. By the time they put doilies and tablecloths over their trunks and boxes and laid reed mats on the dirt floor, the place was quite comfortable.

Their landlord had gossiped to the Spanish-speaking neighbors that the foreigners were accomplished singers. So neighbors began coming to the house asking for concerts. Delighted by the mission field coming to her doorstep, Julia played her autoharp, and she and Ella sang Spanish choruses and hymns. Julia then shared a testimony.

**Last rung on the ladder**

The missionaries discovered that in their local society, the Spanish whites, usually the landowners and merchants, ranked at the top. Next came the mestizos, the mixed Spanish/Indian race, who controlled most of the small businesses in the area. Below them were the cholos, also a mixed race, but farther down economically and socially than the mestizos. And buried at the bottom of the heap were the Quichuas.

Most Quichua families lived in miserable dependance on the haciendas. In exchange for working on the haciendas, the Indian man usually received a small plot of marginal land, the so-called *huasipungo*, to grow enough food to feed his family. Other Quichuas worked on the hacienda so they would be allowed to graze their few sheep or cows on hacienda land. Hacienda foremen often whipped or brutally treated their Quichua laborers. Sometimes they stole the Quichuas' farm animals as a way to make them work extra days to earn back their own animals.

The missionaries' hearts went out to the Quichuas, who by and large were poverty-stricken and malnourished. Almost all suffered from parasites or amoeba infections. Many people had running sores mostly because they did not take baths. Head lice were rampant.

If asked, "How many children do you have?" a Quichua's frequent response was, "Do you mean children living or dead?"

Because of childhood illnesses and inadequate health care, only about half of all Quichua children grew to adulthood. The Quichuas compounded their problems by spending all their money and drinking heavily in the fiestas.

And yet, the Quichuas' spiritual problems were just as serious as their physical ones, the missionaries felt.

After her first three weeks in Caliata, Ella Ozman wrote to the Gospel Missionary Union magazine *The Gospel Message*, "They [the Quichuas] have no hope for eternity, and as we remember that we are the only ones—as far as we know—in all this region who are safe in Christ, we daily long to be able to tell of the Savior to these dear, downtrodden and despised people who are so deep in sin."

## Meeting the priest

The missionaries had been wondering when they would meet the local priest. Then one day they met him on the road. Cordial greetings were exchanged, and the following day the priest's mother paid them a visit. She invited them to her home, only about a mile away, and Julia and Ella went with her that same afternoon.

"Yesterday I told my mother about meeting you two French ladies, and I said she must invite you for a meal," the priest said when they arrived.

"That's very kind of you," Julia said. "But we are from the United States."

"Is that right? Well, that's not important. It's just good to visit with educated people such as yourselves."

The group enjoyed a pleasant conversation. The mother served fresh milk—the missionaries' first since coming to Quichua country—then she took them on a stroll through the garden.

But finally the inevitable question arose about the visitors' religion. And after they answered, the atmosphere cooled considerably.

16

"I suppose they feel they've committed a great sin in being so kind to heretics," Julia said on the way home.

"Yes, but aren't you glad they didn't discover their sin until after serving us that delicious milk?" Ella said.

Both missionaries burst out laughing, and they walked the rest of the way up the mountain arm in arm.

Julia thanked God for the friendship and good working relationship that she and Ella had developed in a few weeks' time. Many Quichuas said they were amazed that two women unrelated by blood could get along so well together in the same house.

Julia and Ella took turns leading devotions every day after breakfast. They chose the book of Genesis to start. "The book of beginnings, appropriate for our work," Ella said.

Each morning after Bible study, they asked God how to use their time for that day. Unless something out of the ordinary happened, they allotted time for visitation and language study. Each day Julia gave Ella a Spanish class; meanwhile, both tried to learn Quichua.

From the first, Ella had talked about the Quichuas as "our people." Unable to speak the language, she still seemed able to communicate. It was Ella who thought of planting a garden. A garden would give them a good point of identification with the Quichua women, she said.

"Ah, fine ladies should not be doing such work," scolded Mamita, seeing the missionaries' grimy hands.

At first Julia felt guilty that she did not share Ella's immediate bond with the Quichuas. In fact, Julia had not really wanted to come here. But soon Julia was forming a love for the Quichuas. When she looked into those black eyes set against high cheekbones, she could see a buried dignity just waiting to be resurrected by the love of Christ.

After a day's tramp through the mountains, Julia and Ella often discussed how best to share Christ with the Quichuas. Oh, for that first convert! The Holy Spirit would have to break down the barriers, they knew.

One month after their arrival in Caliata, one of those barriers raised its ugly head. A still February night erupted

17

with the sound of drums and wild singing. Julia went over to rouse Mamita Cruz.

"This is Carnival," Mamita said, perturbed at being awakened. "Didn't you know? "Don't go out during the next week. You won't enjoy it."

## Bitter cup

Early the next morning Julia went outside and sat on the mud wall in front of the house. She could see the city of Riobamba down in the valley some fifteen miles away. And Mt. Chimborazo's snowy crest gleamed yellow and orange in the morning sun.

"I will lift up mine eyes unto the hills, from whence cometh my help." The verse came to mind as Julia meditated in the spectacular surroundings of her new home.

Suddenly an eerie moan startled Julia from her reverie. Was someone sick? The noise kept getting louder. And now it sounded like singing. The missionary squinted across a plowed field and picked out a Quichua woman. Obviously drunk, the woman weaved and bobbled in a crazy dance. Somehow in her hippety-hops, the woman kept time with the music she was singing.

Twice the woman careened and fell. The second time she lay still and Julia feared she was hurt. But again she staggered to her feet and resumed her drunken dance as if nothing had happened.

As the inebriated woman drew closer, Julia got a better look at her. Why, she had a baby on her back! She would kill it in her falls!

At breakfast, Julia shared her horror. "Imagine. If people are this drunk at dawn, what will it be like towards evening?"

"Maybe Mamita Cruz is right," Ella said. "It might be wise to stay close to home until Carnival is over."

The two missionaries discussed this possibility and then prayed. No, they must go ahead with visitation as usual. A few drunks must not stop this ministry that God had entrusted them.

18

Yet as they walked towards the center of Caliata, Julia and Ella immediately realized this was not a matter of a few, but scores of drunks. Inebriated men and women littered the roadside like casualties of war. Quichua wives sat patiently beside the prone bodies of their husbands, fanning away the flies and waiting until the men awoke from their stupor.

Ella gasped as a blood-soaked man swerved toward them. A reddened cloth wrapped his head in mummy fashion. Almost unconsciously, the missionaries found themselves walking closer together for protection.

Men, who had been friendly before, looked at Julia and Ella with glazed eyes. They leered, taunted and spouted obscenities.

"Don't even look at them," Julia said under her breath to Ella.

Even children, innocent youngsters like the ones who taught them Quichua words on the mountainsides, drank bowlfuls of *chicha*. Did the children get drunk too?

Back home, the missionaries once again asked Mamita Cruz more questions about the feasts. "I told you not to go out," she scolded them. "Carnival is a time when people let loose. They take revenge and make a lot of noise, all the while drinking themselves sick."

Carnival took place during the last four days before Lent, Julia learned. It was the time of penitence and apparently a last chance for sinning before Holy Week.

During the remaining days of Carnival, the missionaries heard the incessant beating of drums and singing. One morning, men dressed in brightly-colored women's shawls and handkerchiefs came to their door demanding *chicha*. It was the custom that every family make the fermented drink for Carnival and serve it to anyone who dropped by.

Julia and Ella were relieved when Carnival ended. However, they soon realized that heavy drinking also figured at funerals, weddings, housebuildings—even a son's ceremonial first haircut.

But worse in the estimation of the missionaries, the drinking and feasting were usually tied to religious ceremo-

19

nies in honor of different saints or virgins. Quichua men paid for the privilege of parading one of the statues or images in their names, believing it would bring blessings.

Perhaps more important to the Quichuas, sponsoring a feast meant status in the community. The *alcalde*, or sponsor, typically received an ornamental staff or cane. It was about the only social prestige a Quichua could get. Of course, *not* sponsoring a feast meant the scorn of one's peers.

A fiesta sponsor had to pay for the liquor, food, band and the priest to say the blessing, and that meant going into debt or depleting more than a year's savings. The men sometimes borrowed from mestizo moneylenders at murderous interest rates. If they borrowed from the hacienda bosses, they would be bound even longer to the landlord until they could repay their loan. Then again, a fiesta sponsor could borrow from a fellow Quichua and pay it back when the friend's turn came to sponsor a fiesta. In summary, the fiestas became self-perpetuating.

The canteen owners did not want to curb the fiestas because their livelihood depended upon them. Some mestizo merchants were known to give a Quichua a free drink, knowing just one cup would send the man on a drinking binge. Then the drunken Quichua was liable to be robbed. If he tried to fight back, he risked winding up like the bloody man Julia and Ella had seen in the road. (For a full explanation of the fiestas, see works written by Eileen Maynard and by Blanca Muratorio, listed in the bibliography.)

## Religious barriers

Julia and Ella could not understand why the priests were trying to stop them, the Christian missionaries, instead of the drunken feasts.

But rumors were circulating that the local priest wanted them burned out of their home. It sounded too outrageous to be true, but previously friendly Quichuas were now shying away. Even the talkative Mamita acted a bit sullen and aloof.

"Is something the matter?" Julia asked Mamita one day.

"They are saying at the church that you are heretics," Mamita admitted. "Some people want to burn the house so you will leave."

Julia's thoughts went immediately to the thatched grass roof. "But what do you think?"

Mamita shrugged. "The priest says you are heretics."

"You know that Ella and I only teach what the Bible says," Julia said. "Do you believe we are heretics?"

"You are entitled to your own religion."

One afternoon Julia and Ella came home to find Mamita sprinkling water in their room. The startled woman said she had been hearing strange noises, and neighbors had told her there were evil spirits. To cleanse the room, she had purchased holy water from the priest.

Religious opposition was growing. So when the priest's uncle invited them to lunch one day, the young missionaries figured something was in the works.

# CHURCH PROPERTY

Under any other circumstances, Julia and Ella would have looked forward to a dinner invitation. But the priest's uncle would hardly have invited two Protestant missionaries for hospitality's sake.

The missionaries' suspicions were confirmed when, arriving at their host's dwelling, they saw the familiar man in clerical garb.

"*Buenas tardes*," the priest said, nodding to the missionaries.

"*Buenas tardes, doctor*," answered Julia, using the term of respect accorded to priests in that region. She wondered how this man could appear so cordial, when everyone knew he opposed them.

The priest had brought along two acquaintances from Riobamba. And the uncle had invited two personal friends. That made it six against two, Julia thought.

The dinner party began pleasantly enough. How did the high altitude affect the ladies? Did they miss the United States? Ella tripped over her Spanish several times, and her embarrassed smile lightened the room.

Then, as if signaling an end to the social amenities, the priest cleared his throat. He dabbed his lips with a napkin and pulled a piece of literature from his satchel. Julia's eyes widened at the sight of one of the tracts she and Ella had been distributing.

"I thought you gentlemen would like to see the kind of materials the *Señoritas* are giving to the Indians," he said. Julia felt the blood rushing to her face.

"Actually it's quite attractive," he said, holding up a copy for all to see. "But it's a pity the Indians won't understand it. I have about forty of these the people have brought to me."

Julia fought back her rising indignation. Why, it was common knowledge the priest had demanded that his parishioners bring him the tracts. "Heretical," he called them.

"Maybe it would help if I explained exactly what my companion and I are doing here in Caliata," Julia said, noting how weak and nervous her voice sounded.

She explained they had come to teach the Quichuas the Bible and about salvation through faith in Jesus Christ. "Surely, the doctor wouldn't oppose that?" she asked.

Surprising even herself, Julia boldly rose from her chair and circled the table, giving a Spanish Gospel of John to each of the guests.

"You've already seen the tract. Now I'd like you to see some of the other materials we are using. We always use the Bible as our reference."

Julia then sat down, praying for boldness before adding one last thing.

"My co-worker and I are concerned about a rumor that is circulating in Caliata," she said. Risking a glance at the priest, she continued, "The people say that you, doctor, want us burned out of our home."

"That's a lie," the priest said quickly, as all eyes turned toward him. Recovering his composure, he said, "I'm sorry you ladies paid attention to such stories. Perhaps you still don't know our Indians, who sometimes, shall we say, invent things.

"This is a difficult area of Ecuador in which to work. I wonder if you ladies ever considered living in Guayaquil?"

Several of the men nodded. So Julia felt that if all else failed that afternoon, at least she could give her personal Christian testimony. Here were six intelligent men in front of her.

"Might I read from the Bible?" she asked.

"I suppose that would be . . . ." the priest began.

"Let me read to you about the new birth," Julia said, opening her Bible to John chapter three.

Everyone listened intently to the passage. Afterwards, the priest offered his interpretation. "The new birth that you mentioned refers to infant baptism, I believe," he said.

The uncle, who had been silent during most of the meal, wrinkled his forehead. "In due respect, that doesn't seem to be the case. Jesus was talking to a grown adult, Nicodemus."

Others added their points of view, and the consensus favored Julia's and the uncle's interpretation. What Julia did *not* want was a theological debate.

"Excuse me, gentleman," she said. "Perhaps it would help if I shared with you what this new birth has meant to me personally."

In her best Spanish, Julia described her own conversion experience. Concluding, she said, "So I was born again, so to speak. Jesus changed me into a new person.

"And I feel called by God to share this message of the new birth with the Quichuas."

When Julia finished, her words seemed to hang in the air and no one said anything for a moment. Several sipped at their coffee, long since gone cold. The meal and conversation had lasted nearly four hours.

"Ah, yours was a special case," the priest said finally. Even he seemed touched by Julia's testimony. "All are not so called to serve God."

Sensing the old innuendo that Quichuas, being Indians, were not capable of being used of God, Julia responded, "But what about the poor fishermen of Galilee? The disciples had no more education than the Quichuas. Yet Jesus chose them to build his church."

"Yes, it may be that some poor Indians will be as wonderfully changed as those disciples," the priest conceded. Then there was another silence.

"But you have a hard, trying work ahead of you," he said slowly. "It will take a long time to accomplish anything."

24

When the dinner party ended, one guest whispered a request for more literature. No one returned their Gospels of John. So perhaps they will read them, Julia hoped.

That night, the two missionaries awoke to the sound of shouts outside their door. It's finally going to happen, they thought. The people are going to set fire to the house! Then everything became quiet. A lonely dog howled from somewhere down the mountain.

During devotions the next morning, Ella read from Genesis chapter 28. At verse 16—"Surely the Lord is in this place and I knew it not"—Julia felt convicted.

"Yesterday, when I was afraid of the priest, and last night, when I feared the shouting, I lacked faith just as Jacob did," she wrote in a letter to *The Gospel Message*. "The Lord was with us all the time, and I knew it not.

"Surely God will not leave us, nor permit the enemy to triumph until He shall have accomplished His will in this field, and gathered His church for His name's sake in Caliata."

### Religious foundations

Ecuador, like most of Latin America up to that time, remained a bastion of Roman Catholicism. With a handful of horses and only 180 soldiers, Francisco Pizarro in 1532 launched a campaign that toppled the mighty Inca empire.

The odds were overwhelmingly against him. But Pizarro, certainly not the picture of righteousness, plunged to the heart of the Inca empire in present-day Peru with the blind faith that God was with him and that he had come to announce the true religion to idolatrous Indians.

After Pizarro's murder of the Inca monarch Atahualpa in 1533, Spanish soldiers quickly subdued the rest of the empire. Spanish soldiers were awarded land and given the right to exact labor and tribute from the Indians already living on it.

As part of this arrangement, the landowners promised to see that the Indians received religious instruction and baptism into the Roman Catholic Church. Priests were invited to teach the Indians. And sometimes, even if the people rejected this new teaching, they were forced to accept baptism anyway.

Dominican priest Bartolomé de Las Casas protested the "accept-it-or-else" style of evangelization. He argued that Indians were just as rational as whites or perhaps even more so. He said Catholic missionaries should preach the gospel using gentle persuasion. Then the Indians should be allowed to draw their own conclusions.

Few seemed to listen to Las Casas, however. In 1565 a Spanish viceroy complained that of 300,000 baptized Indians in the Andes, perhaps only forty were true Christians, according to Rubén Paredes in his study of the Protestant movement in Ecuador and Peru. "The rest were as much idolaters as ever," said the viceroy.

Anti-Protestant attitudes went back to the so-called Catholic reformation of the mid-sixteenth century. King Philip II of Spain ordered adherence in the New World to decrees in the 1563 Council of Trent. This meant the prohibition of Bible reading in the language of the people and religious and ideological monopoly in all Spanish colonies of the Americas, according to evangelical church historian Washington Padilla. Non-Catholics were forbidden the right to emigrate to the Spanish colonies, and offices of the Holy Inquisition were established in the New World.

But not everything in Colonial-era Roman Catholicism was negative, Padilla wrote. Catholic missionaries bravely carried their version of the gospel to the farthest corners of the continent. In the jungles and mountains, they faced sometimes hostile tribes. They taught the people about God and how to read and write. They taught farming methods, the arts and personal hygiene to the indigenous peoples.

Through early Catholic missionary efforts, the region did at least "carry in its bosom a seed of the transforming gospel of Jesus Christ," Padilla said.

**"Tutors and natural fathers"**

When Ecuador became an independent nation in 1830,

26

its first constitution named the parish priests as "tutors and natural fathers of the innocent, servile and miserable indigenous race."

Through the years, the established church took its mandate seriously. It received the right to demand tithes from the Indians. Religious workers and their servants would go into the Quichuas' tiny fields and collect every tenth potato. Small wonder then, some Quichuas harvested their potatoes at night, when they would not be seen.

The liberal Alfaro government, which opened Ecuador to Protestant missionaries at the turn of the twentieth century, reduced the church's power. It took away church control of the nation's schools, and civil marriage and burial were instituted.

But as the missionaries discovered, these reforms were not usually observed or enforced in remote areas of the interior.

## Syncretism among Quichuas

Despite their Roman Catholic veneer, many Quichuas still observed many of the old animistic rituals. Julia once saw a man toss a lamb into a deep ravine as a sacrifice to the devil.

"God is good and doesn't need such sacrifices," he told her. "But Satan is a bad, demanding master, who needs to be appeased."

Quichuas sometimes left food sacrifices for Mother Earth. And after a woman gave birth, it was not unusual for the family to bury her placenta by the doorstep for good luck.

Some Quichua medicine men invoked not only God, but the saints, spirits of the dead and even the spirits of animals when administering their potions and treatments. Quichua "healers" often used the *cuy*, or guinea pig. They would pass the animal over the sick person and then kill it and cut the body open. Where the blood settled in the animal's body, that was where they believed the sickness lay. Other

Quichua practitioners, the *sopladores*, attempted to "blow out" the disease.

Quichuas would sometimes blame their illnesses on "bad air," which they had breathed somewhere. Certain places were to be avoided for that reason. Parents often attributed a child's illness to someone giving them the *mal ojo*, the evil eye. Fright could also cause illness, they believed.

These same Quichuas, with their blend of Catholic piety and animistic rituals, seemed confused about the most basic Christian tenets. When Julia asked the Quichuas about Jesus, they sometimes asked to which idol or crucifix she was referring. Some considered heaven a reward for those going to mass, sponsoring the drunken fiestas or even for being exploited by the whites.

"Miss, there is something I have been wanting to ask you," said a sick elderly Quichua named Thomas.

"What is that?" asked Julia, who had been reading him Scripture.

"All these sufferings that God is sending me—will they be received towards saving my soul?"

In a letter to *The Gospel Message*, Julia described the scene. "It is pitiful to see him try to comprehend the gospel, and it is discouraging to me not to be able to make him see the way of salvation. That, however, is God's work.

"His knowledge of the saints, mass, etc., and also what I tell him, confuses him, and he asks, 'But to which shall I pray? Who can hear best?' And then he asks what to pray—'The creed, the Lord's prayer, Hail Mary or some other?'"

Many Quichuas had great faith in the saints but none in Christ, Julia complained once in a letter to *The Gospel Message*.

"A young man told us recently of the usefulness of saints," she wrote. "For instance, for a blessing on his cattle he must invoke Saint Mark; on the pigs, Saint Anthony; on the sheep, Saint John.

"If he wants a good wife who will not drink or be troublesome to him, Saint Joseph is the one he must ask to pick her out for him; and to procure the favor, he must put a lighted candle before the image of Joseph. I never hear them say they must pray to Christ, or speak of the love of Christ.

"Oh! how glorious it will be when His love dawns on their hearts . . . and they behold Him with the veil lifted from their darkened eyes. May God hasten that time and glorify His Son among our Quichua people."

If the Quichuas were going to find God's truth, they must get the Scriptures in their own language, Julia determined. The Bible-reading Quichua would see God's plan of salvation.

Accordingly, Julia threw her attentions into learning the language. Within eighteen months' time, she could speak some verses in Quichua and carry on simple conversations. Ella had sufficiently mastered the Spanish so that now she could begin working with Julia on learning Quichua—an exciting prospect.

During this time, Julia and Ella attended a GMU conference in Guayaquil. And two more missionaries accompanied them back to Chimborazo—Lela Easley and Amy Ward, who planned to start a permanent work in the provincial capital, Riobamba.

Julia could hardly wait to get home to Caliata—a sharp contrast to eighteen months before, when she had had misgivings about going to the Quichuas. Now, things were looking up. Surely, God would work among the Quichuas soon.

# 5

# I HEAR INDIANS SINGING

The train from Guayaquil ran only as far as the village of Guamote, but the four missionaries felt they had gotten their money's worth.

The trip had lasted twelve hours—the steam engine chugging 125 miles through banana and sugar plantations, the gorgeous Andes Mountains and a series of switchbacks on nearly perpendicular Devil's Nose Ridge. The women arrived in Guamote exhausted, but the train was still better than traveling by road. Before the track recently opened, the same trip overland had taken at least a week.

The next morning the missionaries rented horses for the final leg of their journey into Caliata. A full day's journey of fifteen miles awaited them, and the missionaries set out eagerly. But a cold rain quickly dampened their zeal.

"Oh, this trail is terrible," they said almost in unison.

The downpour had turned the dust to mud, and the horses slipped and slid on the trail. Peering into the deep gorges beside the trail, Ella Ozman decided it would be safer to walk alongside her animal until the trail became more sure. She dismounted under protests from the rest. Before long, sweat rolled from her forehead, and she was gasping for breath in the thin air.

When Ella could walk no further, she remounted. Sharp gusts of wind pierced the missionaries' thick clothing, and

Ella, because she had been sweating, chilled worse than the others. By the time the group finally reached Caliata, she trembled uncontrollably.

"You'd better get out of those clothes and into bed," Julia told her.

The next morning Ella awoke with pneumonia symptoms. All day, she had hot and cold chills. Then before evening, she fell into a coma. Julia knew something had to be done—and fast.

"Lela and Amy, stay here with Ella while I try to find a doctor," she ordered.

Julia threw on a coat and headed out the door. Lela Easley and Amy Ward appeared dazed by their rude introduction to mountain missionary work.

Urgency pushed Julia forward in a three-mile walk through the dark and mud. Finally she found someone willing to ride to Riobamba for the doctor. It would be morning at least before the doctor could come, so Julia silently prayed that God would speed his journey.

That night the women tried to remain cheerful. They alternated daubing Ella's forehead with a wet rag and maintained a prayer vigil around her bed.

As night drifted toward morning, Julia suggested that the other two get some rest. She would stay up with Ella. They objected, but Julia secretly wanted to be alone for a few moments with her friend.

The candle flickered in the dark room and sent wild shadows onto the mud wall. Julia knelt beside the bed.

"Please heal her," Julia cried out to the Lord. "Ella loves the Quichuas. You brought her here."

The messenger to Riobamba arrived late the next afternoon. "The doctor said you can either take the sick woman to Riobamba or, for twenty-five sucres, he will come out tomorrow."

There was no need for a decision, however. Five minutes before the messenger arrived, Ella had regained consciousness for an instant. She seemed to recognize her anxious friends. Her eyes glanced upward and a look of surprised joy crossed her face. Then she died.

## Burial for a "heretic"

Julia had no time to grieve or reflect. Arrangements had to be made. She collected her thoughts, deciding to take the body to the home of a nearby Spanish acquaintance.

Julia went on ahead to see about having a coffin made and about a place to bury Ella. She had to borrow a steel bar for the gravediggers, and she carried it across her lap on the way to the village of Licto.

However, Licto officials refused burial in their cemetery to a Protestant "heretic." So Julia rode on to Riobamba, where authorities had set aside a corner in the local cemetery for suicide victims, religious heretics and the like.

Amy and Lela went slowly on horses behind the corpse, which several Quichua men had tied to a bed and carried on their shoulders. Once in Riobamba, the tiny funeral procession made its way toward the cemetery.

Passersby commented among themselves, but purposely loud enough for the missionaries to hear, "You see, that is what happens to Protestants."

The words smacked into Julia like buckshot. "Years ago, when we counted the cost for becoming missionaries, we knew we would be jeered at and continually misjudged," Julia had said once. Now those words were coming true.

Julia, Lela and Amy stood numbly at the far end of the cemetery. Wind flicked at the page as Julia read one of Ella's favorite Scriptures. Amy and Julia sang a hymn, and Julia said a few words. They prayed, and it was all over. The impatient gravediggers, glad to finish their job, lowered the casket into the hole.

For the next several days, Julia stayed in Riobamba— glad for the company of Lela and Amy at this difficult time. Inwardly, she questioned God, "Why? Why did you call Ella away just when she seemed ready to do more than ever in ministry to the Quichuas?"

## Home to an empty house

When she returned alone to Caliata, Julia dreaded the

thought of an empty house. Surely, the whites would whisper that Ella's death was a judgment from God. Her mestizo and cholo friends would probably feel the same, but be too kind to say anything.

Mt. Chimborazo looked cruelly beautiful that day on the ride home. The Puruhás had offered human sacrifices to the mountain, and Julia felt as if the snowy peak had snatched away another victim, missionary Ella Ozman.

Her spirits sank even lower as the horse climbed the last stretch into Caliata. Seeing Julia, several Quichua men ran toward her. "Welcome back, *niña* Julia," the men said, using the more affectionate address, *niña* or girl, than *doña* or *señorita*.

"Why...thank-you," mumbled Julia, surprised.

"*Niña* Ella went straight to heaven," said one, kindly implying that Ella had not needed the purifying fires of purgatory before reaching heaven.

Again, Julia was touched. "Yes, Ella is in heaven with her Lord," she said.

The missionary felt like hugging the Quichuas for their unexpected kindness. At the same time, she sensed a deep emptiness. There were no born-again Christians here with whom to "unload" and share with on a deep spiritual level.

Outside the house, Mamita Cruz sat weeping. The old woman had been a special prayer burden of Ella's.

"Now, who will sit by my side when I am alone?" she lamented. "And who will read me those pretty Bible stories and give me hot drinks when I am ill?"

Julia patted Mamita's hand and ducked inside the house. Ella's belongings lay untouched. "Now, who will sit by my side when I am alone?" Julia thought.

Suddenly all the pent-up agony and tension of the previous days tumbled out in tears. Julia sat on the bed. The air was damp, the house drab and her heart cold. If only her former pastor Will Reed or any other Christian friend were here.

Julia's eyes fell on her Bible. She mindlessly flicked it open and found herself reading Psalm 77. "In the day of my trouble I sought the Lord...My soul refused to be comforted," it began.

The words seemed to describe her, and Julia found herself reading ahead.

"I remembered God, and was troubled: I complained, and my spirit was overwhelmed." Again, she identified.

"Will the Lord cast off forever? And will he be favorable no more? Is his mercy clean gone for ever? Doth his promise fail for evermore?"

Julia began reading faster to see how the Psalmist resolved his dilemma, so much like her own.

"I will remember the works of the Lord," wrote the Psalmist. "Surely I will remember thy wonders of old...Who is so great as our God? Thou art the God that doest wonders."

When she finished reading, Julia Anderson sensed God had spoken directly to her and her situation. She remembered that life's problems come and go, but God's goodness never changes.

Her God, the great God who does wonders, would do them again—in her life and also among the Quichuas. At that moment, peace entered Julia's spirit—quietly, unnoticed, as if through the back door.

That evening Julia shared her difficult lessons and experiences of the preceding days in a letter to *The Gospel Message*. She confessed to her lack of prayer and said she had relied too much on her own strength and effort in ministry to the Quichuas. She promised God she would remain faithful in ministry as long as He gave her strength.

"At times I think of the future," Julia wrote, "and I fancy that I can see souls saved and hear Indians singing the Gospel.

"Then I cannot but wonder who will be the first, and when: if it may be that my own eyes shall see and enjoy such blessedness as a worker among them, or if, like Moses, I must see it as from a distance and let others be partakers of its joy."

How prophetic that statement would be!

## More trials coming

The death of co-worker Ella Ozman became only the first in a succession of Job-like trials for Julia Anderson. The following year she contracted smallpox. She survived, but the disease scarred her face. The young missionary later confessed that it was months before God gave her the victory over self-consciousness.

Other single female workers joined her during the next ten or fifteen years, but the missionaries faced a lonely struggle amid religious fanatics and listeners who were not interested.

"We were the only Christians, the only lights. And we felt that our light shone too dimly," Julia wrote.

Before long, Julia's taxing labors began taking their toll.

"In rather poor health physically, the altitude got me, nerves and mind as well as bodily weakness," she later wrote.

"Yet as I kept going, new strength was given me for long walks into valleys and up mountains and often with poor food, and as a rule rejoicing in God, but again yielding to discouragement, even despair.

"Should have had more frequent changes to the coast—years with no change not good physically, spiritually or mentally. There was so much 'confusion' in my head when weak, and I had fainting spells and often feared insanity but seemed to need to stay on: 'Day by day the manna fell.'"

Julia was sometimes asked to teach Spanish to new GMU missionaries to Ecuador. She and one of her students, missionary William Woodward, fell in love and got married in 1915.

William Woodward's fragile health did not permit him to spend long periods in the high altitude of Chimborazo. So the newlyweds started working mostly on the coast in Guayaquil. This upset George Fisher, who wanted Julia in full-time Quichua work. So in obedience to her field director, Julia started leaving her husband to spend long periods of time in Caliata. Because of the expense, they mutually agreed that he would not travel to visit her.

During World War I, Ecuadorian missionaries' support money arrived only sporadically. To make ends meet, Julia sometimes sold dishes out of the cupboard or made shirts to sell to the Quichuas. Once she lived for two weeks on okas, a mountain vegetable, and salt. The financially strapped missionary couple decided not even to write to each other because of the cost of stamps.

The periods of separation were hard to bear. Years later Julia told a friend, "I don't think the Lord asked that of me." During these years, the Woodwards also lost a son in childbirth.

In 1926, the couple took a furlough—Julia's first, after twenty-eight years in Ecuador. During Julia's physical exam at Mayo Clinic, the doctor found traces of tuberculosis and said that her move in 1902 from coastal Guayaquil to high-altitude Chimborazo had probably saved her life.

That was encouraging news—evidence of God's providence. But then another hard blow fell. Mr. Woodward died suddenly, apparently of a heart attack as he knelt in prayer at his bedside. And Julia Anderson Woodward again returned alone to Quichua country.

The decades passed: the 1930s, 1940s and into the 1950s. Sometimes the Quichua ministry showed hope. But each time things looked up, the opposition rose in a fury.

Once religious fanatics swept through Caliata. They gathered all the Christian literature the missionaries had distributed and burned it in front of the Catholic church. They also threatened to take Julia forcibly to mass. For a long time after this, her Quichua friends were too frightened even to greet Julia in public.

Children occasionally professed faith in the Bible during literacy classes, which Julia maintained in her home. But most were pressured back into their old ways.

One new Quichua convert hid in the loft of his home during Carnival, coming down only to eat. The man's friends found him during his fourth day of hiding, and they forced a first drink down the recovering alcoholic's throat. That was like touching a match to gas. He started drinking again and left the church entirely.

Julia suspected there were some secret believers— Quichuas who had trusted Christ but never publicly declared their faith for fear of persecution. Several Quichuas made deathbed confessions. Certain others, because of their evangelical convictions, refused last rites from a priest. But in terms of lasting visible results, Julia Woodward and her co-workers made little headway.

Evangelical missions in general faced a tough time. In 1925—after almost thirty years of Protestant missions— Ecuador had only 158 evangelical believers, said evangelical church historian Washington Padilla. By 1945—after nearly a half century of Protestant missions—Ecuador had only 5,000 baptized Protestant believers and a worshiping community of 13,000.

Once someone asked Julia, "How can you carry on out there without anyone accepting the Lord?"

"The greater the darkness, the more need there is of light," she said. She sometimes quoted, "He hath not taught us to trust in His name, and thus far brought us, to bring us to shame."

At least the translation work gave Mrs. Woodward reason for hope. She was convinced that Quichuas would turn to Christ once they began reading God's Word in their mother tongue.

The translation work, which involved a few other GMU workers such as Dora Regier, who in 1950 pioneered a GMU mission station among the Quichuas in the village of Pulucate, also gave Mrs. Woodward an outlet. At least in translating the Quichua New Testament, she could see measurable progress.

## Quichua New Testament finished

At age seventy-one Julia Woodward completed her New Testament translation, a bilingual Quichua/Spanish version.

The manuscript was sent to the American Bible Society in 1949, and published copies reached Chimborazo Quichuas in 1954—a year after Julia's retirement from full-time missionary service. The American Bible Society gave Mrs. Woodward special recognition for her lifelong translation effort.

Before leaving Ecuador, Mrs. Woodward was honored at a special going-away service. The veteran missionary had dreaded what she called the "ordeal" of being in the spotlight, but she turned out enjoying it. "It would almost be worth living here another fifty years to get such a send-off," she quipped to the audience's delight.

She was presented a gold medal with her life's verse, Romans 10:11, inscribed upon it.

Four days before her trip home to the U.S., Julia wrote, "I weigh 139 pounds, and I have pretty high blood pressure. But the doctor says it's perfectly safe to fly. We don't go over 10,000 feet high."

But her homeward flight became one last trial. Mrs. Woodward packed nearly all her earthly possessions in two battered suitcases and a tote bag. But somehow the suitcases were lost between Miami, Florida, and mission headquarters in Kansas City, Missouri.

"We put tracers on those bags for two years," said Mrs. Don Shidler of GMU. "Everything she owned, including invaluable pictures of her husband and work, original translation manuscripts, her diaries and clothing—all perished."

Mrs. Woodward received little acclaim back home in the United States. When she left Ecuador after more than fifty years' service, Mrs. Woodward said, "I can count on one hand the number of Quichuas I am sure to see in heaven."

When would the spiritual harvest come? Would it ever?

# THE ORDINARY LAYMAN

New missionary to Ecuador Henry Klassen had known for a long time God wanted him in overseas Christian work, but it proved hard getting there.

Few missions wanted someone like him—a man who had quit school in the seventh grade to work on his father's farm, and who maybe knew more about tending cattle than teaching theology.

Henry and three other classmates at Briercrest Bible Institute in Canada had arranged a private meeting with a mission agency representative. They wanted to find out more about becoming missionaries.

"Please tell me a little about yourselves," the missions official began the meeting.

Each of the four students came from a rural background. Bible institute was their first formal training. After listening to the group, the man gathered his papers and snapped shut his briefcase.

"I would suggest all of you stay on the farm. You'll be much happier there," he said.

He thanked the students and left.

Henry was not going to give up that easily. He traced his missionary calling back as far as grade school on the prairies of Manitoba, Canada. A missionary had told Henry's class about the sick, hungry children in Africa. It felt like God was tugging him to go help them.

"Why pick on me, God?" Henry thought at the time. "I'm not even a Christian yet."

After Henry did become a Christian, again it was a missionary who pricked his conscience.

"Henry, don't you think God has something better for you than working in a meat-packing plant for the rest of your life?" the missionary said.

Henry thought and prayed about that for awhile, and he decided God did have something better for him. The strapping, 180-pounder quit his well-paying job at a Winnipeg meat-packing plant and made plans to attend Briercrest Bible Institute in Caronport, Saskatchewan. His superiors said he was foolish for leaving. They liked his work and offered him first, higher pay, and then a foreman's job, if he would stay. But Henry could not go against what he felt to be God's will.

Henry felt led to Latin America. At Briercrest, an endless stream of visiting missionaries and speakers whetted the students' vision for missions. One of these, Don Shidler of Gospel Missionary Union, told about the need for more missionaries to the Quichua Indians of Ecuador.

Something clicked in Henry's mind when he heard it. Afterward, he could not even remember the details of the message.

But his impression was, "Here are country people, people like me. They just need somebody to go out there and live with them and love them."

Henry felt a kinship with the Quichuas even though he had never seen or met them. He must talk with Shidler. But would the mission accept him? He still felt the bruises from his last encounter with a mission agency official.

And what did Pat think?

"About what?" asked his bride-to-be, when Henry saw her in the dining hall. She never knew whether Henry, an incorrigible tease, was joking or serious, so she was going to play it safe.

"What did you think of the talk about the Quichua Indians?" Henry asked.

"It's funny. I barely know where Ecuador is, but his mes-

40

sage really spoke to me."

"Do you mean it?" Henry pursued.

"I was interested in what he said about them being descendants of the Incas—people who had worshiped the sun, but when they saw that even a cloud could cover its power, they knew there had to be a Higher Being."

"Yeah, and they still don't know that Jesus is who they're really looking for," said Henry, enthused because Pat seemed to have the same feeling about the Quichuas that he did. "What would you think if we went as missionaries to the Quichuas?"

Pat laughed. "Is this another proposal of marriage?"

"Maybe," grinned Henry.

Pat still teased him for never having really asked for her hand in marriage. At the end of their first school term, he had approached his sweetheart with the question, "Would you go to South America with me?" Of course, she wanted to marry him, but that was a pretty funny way to propose, she thought. It was almost as creative as the way Henry had introduced himself to her when he managed to trip her on the ice-skating rink and pick her up before her partner could.

Before the GMU representative left Briercrest, both Henry and Pat had a chance to meet with him. Shidler assured them their Christian ministry experiences would count as much as their academic ones. They filled out applications and were accepted.

The couple got married in Kelowna, Pat's home town in British Columbia, right after their graduation. Henry sold his car so they would have enough money for train fare to the GMU missionary candidates school in Kansas City.

## Making friends

Upon arrival in Ecuador in 1953, the Klassens visited the Caliata mission station before going to Shell Mera in the jungle for language study.

Henry felt encouraged by his weekend in Caliata. Someone had told him Quichuas never smiled. But the Quichua

41

women there had not stopped giggling at the sight of him and Pat—a bit disconcerting, perhaps, but also a good sign. "I don't think it will be so hard to make friends with the Quichuas," he told Pat.

While he might not have had a long list of academic credentials or a specialized skill, Henry felt at least he had the gift or the ability to make friends. He just plain loved getting to know people...what they did for a living, what they thought about, how they lived.

People could tell Henry liked them, so when he shared about his very best friend, Jesus Christ, they paid attention.

Henry became the mission's first man in full-time Quichua work. He and Pat joined a contingent of nine single female missionaries, who were pleased to have a handyman like Henry around. He could fix those broken appliances and leaky pipes the single women had been worrying about.

"How do you know so much?" one of the women asked him.

"I just know what I learned on the farm," he said. "My Dad always told me, 'You keep your eyes open and learn from what others are doing.'"

Henry had worked in logging camps, a fruit-packing plant, in maintenance work, Christian camping, as well as on the farm, so he had plenty of experience to draw from.

There was something about him that bespoke stability and common sense. He did not get rattled when things went wrong. If there was a problem, Henry said, there had to be a practical solution. If you didn't know how to do something, then plunge in and learn it.

The Klassens had no sooner arrived in Ecuador than people started warning against going to the Quichua work.

"It's cold up there—physically, as well as spiritually," said a fellow missionary.

"You'll be wasting your time," said another. "Why don't you work on the coast where people are more responsive?"

If anything, those discouraging comments had just the opposite effect upon Henry. God would not let fifty years of ministry among the Quichuas go to waste. There had to be a way to reach the Quichuas with the gospel.

"Maybe I sound like a brash young missionary," Henry confided to Pat, "but I don't buy the idea that it's sufficient if we as missionaries only sow the seed."

"What do you mean?"

"If the Quichuas aren't accepting the gospel the way we're working now, then maybe some changes have to be made."

But during nine months of Spanish study and then another several months in Caliata, Henry spent more time trying to learn two new languages and cultures than he did plotting changes in mission strategy.

Then word came that the mission had bought a property in the village of Majipamba. Would Henry and Pat move there and open a GMU mission station? Henry did not have to think twice before accepting.

## Starting in Colta

The Seventh-Day Adventists opened the first mission station in Majipamba in 1918. Then the Christian and Missionary Alliance (C&MA) bought it from them and had just as much trouble making inroads among the Quichuas.

Finally, the C&MA decided to sell the station. And GMU bought it largely because of its location—being centrally located between its stations in Riobamba, Caliata and the recently opened one in the village of Pulucate.

Seemingly, the station had possibilities. It sat beside the Pan American Highway and the railroad running between Quito and Guayaquil, so lots of people passed by every day. Henry wondered why the Adventists and the Alliance, which both had operated a clinic and a school there, never succeeded in forming a Quichua church.

While Pat was in Quito awaiting the birth of their second child, Henry roamed the surrounding mountains with a Spanish C&MA worker, Matías Mogrovejo, who stayed on to help him get oriented.

The two men walked miles. Matías introduced Henry to Quichuas he knew, and Henry wrote down new Quichua vocabulary words in the notebook he always carried. At the start, he was not so concerned about getting the grammar right, but he wanted to at least know what the words meant. In a matter of weeks, Henry had a list of 500 new words, which he tried to memorize and put to use. His outgoing personality proved a boon to language study. When Pat asked how he had learned Quichua so fast, Henry said, "I just use what I know. I ask the Quichuas about their animals, their crops, the weather, anything."

Henry also asked Matías plenty of questions as they worked together, making the mud-walled house liveable for a wife, an infant son, and a new baby.

"Don't try to reach the old folks—that's hopeless," Matías counseled. "Work with the younger generation."

Partly for that reason, the Klassens decided to keep going the school on the property. This was a major priority as soon as Pat arrived in Majipamba, or Colta, as it was generally called, with new baby daughter Beverley.

However, the school ended a dismal failure. The mestizo pupils picked on their Quichua classmates. Even worse, a local priest threatened to fine any Quichua parents who sent their children there. By year's end, attendance had dropped from fifty to twenty-three and only three of those were Quichuas. The Klassens saw they had lots to learn.

Henry continued making contacts on foot and on a bicycle which he had purchased. Also, the Quichuas came to them—just as they had to Julia Woodward—wanting medicines and medical treatment. Henry was willing to help, but he flatly told the Quichuas he was not a medical doctor. His only medical training consisted of a few short lessons from a medical missionary. He and other GMUers practiced stitching wounds on pieces of beef and giving injections to oranges.

But the Quichuas kept coming anyway. Once, men brought Henry a friend, whose foot had been smashed by a railroad car.

"You'd better take this man to the hospital in Riobamba," said Klassen, somewhat queasy at the sight of the mangled flesh.

"What? Take him to those horse doctors?" they said.

44

Apparently, the Spanish doctors neglected or took advantage of Quichuas, so the latter would rather take their chances on Henry, inexperience notwithstanding.

Many times, Henry gulped, prayed and treated wounds that looked too serious for him to handle. But it was amazing how much good a little washing and penicillin could do.

He and Pat often treated victims of the fiestas, such as the man whose hand was blown off by fiesta fireworks or the people suffering multiple machete or knife wounds. The Klassens received patients in a small anteroom they had set up in their house. Pat often cleansed the wounds for Henry, and she found particularly horrifying the number of people with scabies, a very irritating skin disease. Even babies got it, and they were brought to her with faces raw and red from scratching.

Matías had left behind a pair of rusty forceps, and Henry found himself pulling teeth. When a husband brought in his ailing wife, Henry couldn't even touch her infected molar—it was so sensitive.

"I'm going to get hold of that tooth good and solid," he thought, grabbing it with his pliers.

The woman shrieked in pain and gripped Henry's arm, pulling as she did. The tooth came out at the same time. But she passed out onto the floor. Henry ran after a glass of water, and she regained consciousness.

"Well, aren't you going to pull it?" she asked.

"I already did," said Henry, showing her the tooth. She stuck a dirty finger into the vacant space and realized that he had.

## Putting in a cemetery

Quichuas also requested Klassen's help with legal transactions. The Spanish authorities overcharged or took advantage of them and Henry was surprised how matters sped along for the Quichuas in the government offices if a white man like him happened to be there.

One legal obstacle involved cemeteries. Henry knew the

only government-recognized graveyards fell under Catholic jurisdiction, and Protestant burials usually were not permitted. The Quichuas regarded a religious burial as very important, Henry found out. So if they could not get a decent burial, they would hardly want to become evangelicals.

Accordingly, Henry wrangled with authorities for permission to put in a cemetery on mission property. Finally, they granted permission but with the stipulation that only foreigners or missionaries could be buried there.

"That defeats the entire purpose," Henry said, going once more to the authorities.

"Didn't we give you the permission you wanted?"

"Yes, but it doesn't help the Quichuas who become evangelicals." This was getting frustrating to Henry. "Do you want them to bury their dead in their backyards or in the ravines or in some other illegal place?"

"No, that wouldn't be good," agreed an official. He promised to do what he could.

In two weeks, an amended permission came back. It allowed the burial of the foreigners *and* those who followed their teachings. When this news got around, Henry noticed a new appreciation for him on the part of the Quichuas. He got the feeling they knew he really cared.

As much as possible, Henry tried to identify with his Quichua neighbors. He planted a garden and raised a pig. When someone stole the potatoes from Henry's patch, the neighbors felt closer to the missionary.

"You mean, they even steal *your* potatoes, *doctorcito*?"

The Klassens added a third member to their family, a baby boy, Cecil, and they found that having three fair-headed youngsters around opened many conversations with admiring Quichuas.

Henry understood that in order to get a hearing for the gospel, he must earn the Quichuas' friendship and respect. If that meant treating sick people, fighting city hall or even raising pigs, he would try.

46

# 7

# THE TRUST FACTOR

Henry Klassen had arrived in Colta the same year Julia Woodward left the Ecuadorian mission field: 1953.

"Things haven't changed among the Quichuas for years," the C&MA worker Matías had said.

"They are just the same as when *Señorita* Julia arrived. The Incas probably did more to change the Quichuas' culture in just a few years than the Spanish have in four centuries."

It sounded amazing to Henry, but apparently it was true. The other missionaries had told him about Julia Woodward's troubles. The same barriers to the gospel that had blocked her—the feasts, the religious opposition and the discrimination against Quichuas—still faced him and the other GMU missionaries. If anything, the barriers had grown taller.

As to the feasts in Colta, the Klassens' ministry completely deteriorated in September. The harvest feasts began at one end of the lake during the first week. Then the partyers moved to several other villages around the lake on succeeding weeks. The wild parades, drinking, and noisemaking lasted the entire month, and it was hardly safe to go out.

Henry got his first taste of religious opposition one Sunday when he sold Bibles and Christian literature in the market at nearby Cajabamba. He had asked the city officials' permission, and they told him, "Go right ahead. There's no

47

law against it. Nobody will want to accept your literature, though."

Things went smoothly until one Sunday a stern woman warned Henry that if he came back the next week, her Catholic league would stop him by force.

Henry and Pat prayed a lot that week. Henry felt tempted to take the mission's 1939 Ford pickup the following Sunday to Cajabamba, but he decided to trust the Lord and go by bicycle as usual.

He had no sooner arrived in town, when men stepped out of two houses and grabbed his handlebars.

"What right do you have as a foreigner to hand out subversive literature?" they demanded.

For a moment, Henry lost his nerve. Were they going to beat him up? Then he remembered God's ever-present protection.

"I'll go with you to the police chief if you have a complaint," he said, composed once again.

"Our orders come from a higher authority than one in the land," one man replied.

That comment opened a door for witness as wide as a truck. Henry preached for twenty minutes to the most attentive crowd he had ever had. Then he politely asked to be excused. The men released his bike, and Henry rode back to Colta praising the Lord.

A Quichua boy told Henry the next day, "I talked with one of the attackers. He told me he still doesn't know why he didn't beat you up. He even lost out on the pay he was going to get for doing the job."

## Centuries of distrust

Klassen and the other missionaries sometimes found themselves in a rather delicate position between the Spanish whites and the Quichuas. Klassen wanted to defend the Quichuas from the abuses by Spanish whites. At the same time, he did not want to alienate himself from the whites— he had friends among them, too. As a foreigner, Klassen many times felt like he was outside of things.

Klassen had always championed the underdog, and he could not fathom how certain Spanish whites could hate and so badly mistreat the Quichuas. Once he saw a bus driver shouting for a waiting Quichua to get inside. The man explained he was waiting for his family who had not arrived yet. The driver snatched off the Quichua's hat and threw it on top of the bus.

"If you want your hat, you'd better get in," the driver said.

As the Quichua scrambled aboard to retrieve his hat, the vehicle took off, and the Quichua had to pay his bus fare. Henry could not believe what he had seen. "Do you really think that man is ever going to ride your bus again?" he asked the driver.

Another time, a visiting friend from North America had gone below the mission station to watch the barley harvest.

"Just be careful," Henry warned, knowing what his friend might see.

In a short time, the friend burst back into the house.

"Where's your gun, Henry?"

"Just hold on a minute. What's the matter?"

Down below, the work boss had just run over an old Quichua woman with his horse because she had not carried her heavy load of barley fast enough, the friend said angrily. Henry tried to calm him. Guns wouldn't do any good, he said.

"But doesn't it bother you?" the friend spluttered.

"Of course, it bothers me. It's maddening, in fact. But as foreigners and as missionaries, we just can't go running in with guns and taking things into our own hands. This has been going on for centuries."

The discrimination against Quichuas caused them to draw inside themselves and distrust any outsiders, Henry realized. During his first year in Chimborazo, Henry tried to help a Quichua man he found bleeding to death along the road. Instead of being grateful, the Quichua immediately asked what the missionary wanted from him: Any white man showing kindness to a Quichua must have an ulterior motive.

In his walks through the mountains, Henry became a little perturbed that Quichuas always addressed him as *doctorcito* or with some other term of respect.

Finally, he told some Quichuas, "Look at me. I'm wearing an old hat, an old poncho, and I eat and sleep where you do. Why do you address me differently than your own people?"

A Quichua man answered, "Look at your glasses. How many Quichuas do you see wearing glasses? Second, you're taller than us. And we also know where you came from."

So winning the Quichuas' trust became one of Klassen's biggest battles. Complicating things, some of the Spanish whites' religious leaders made the Quichuas afraid of the missionaries by claiming that the foreigners had come to take the Quichuas' blood or that they "ate people's flesh."

Nearly two years passed before Henry felt like he could discuss matters of the heart with a Quichua.

## Protective shells

At an inter-mission prayer meeting, Klassen heard Eugene Nida of the American Bible Society say, "The Quichuas have built protective shells around themselves.

"There are layers of superstition, self-preservation, fear, fatalism, isolation, and prejudice. You've got to penetrate these before you can get to the Quichuas' hearts where the gospel will strike home."

Hearing Nida's comments, Henry inwardly vowed to break through those layers with God's help.

Sitting one day in Colta with grandfather Pacho, Henry decided to probe.

"Pacho, you've heard the gospel many times," Henry said. "You've been friendly to us. Why don't you accept?"

"Our ancestors had a religion, which was replaced by one the Spaniards brought and forced upon us. We've learned to live with that one. I'm too old to change my religion now. Besides, there would be too much opposition."

The old man fell silent. Henry could see there was no use

One of the early "pioneers," Dora Regier 1954, was faithful through the difficult years despite persecution and threats on her life. (*photo: Henry Klassen*)

In the foreground is the original church in El Troje, the first church building for the Quichuas. (*photo: John Maust*)

Left page top: Early co-workers: Mabel Alton, Edith Kruse, Julia Woodward and Jean Mann, 1940.

Left page bottom: Julia Woodward outside her Caliata home in the 1940s with some students.

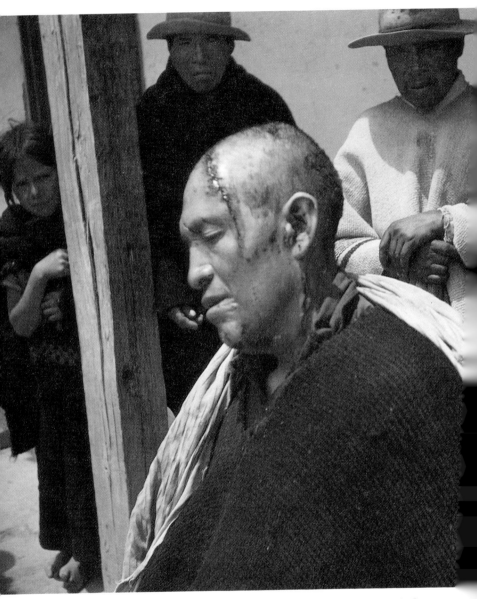

Treating head wounds at the Caliata clinic, 1958. (*photo: Henry Klassen*)

Mary Warkentin (top, at left) and Roberta Hostetter, for many years, part of the "Quichua team." (*photo: John Maust*)

Joyce Benston and Manuel Naula collaborate on translation projects. (*photo: Don Dixon*)

Matias Mullo standing beside the 30-foot deep ditch into which persecutors threw him. (*photo: John Maust*)

Right page top: Joyce Benston (left) and Christine Burt sell Bibles and Scripture portions to eager Quichua readers, 1976. (*photo: Charles Brents*)

Right page bottom: Julia Woodward presents the first copy of the Quichua New Testament to GMU president, Don. P. Shidler, in 1954.

Mass baptisms in cold mountain streams were common occurrences during the "revival in the Andes."

Bible conferences and evangelistic campaigns attract mass audiences. (*photos: Carl McMindes*)

Quichua leader Basilio Malán (bottom right) greets Ecuadorioan president Rodgriguez Lara(bottom left) during the president's visit to Majipamba in 1975. ( *photo: Charles Brents*)

Mary Warkentine, Manuel Bahua Cajas (center) and Manuel Naula Sagnay organize the translation of Old Testament Bible stories. (*photo: Charles Brents*)

Henry Klassen overlooking the river where 155 believers in San Bernardo were baptized. (*photo: John Maust*)

Music plays a large role in Quichua life and worship. (*photo: Verlan Smith*)

Facing page left: Life has changed little for the Quichua "cowboys" of the Andean highlands. (*photo: Carl McMindes*)

Below: Jos Mari Yukilema is proud to see his language in print. (*photo: Henry Klassen*)

Basilio Malán (*photo: John Maust*)

The translation team for the Quichua Old Testament. (*photo: John Maust*)

Henry Klassen and the author received hospitably at the former Caliata station.

Henry and Pat Klassen—a life-time
commitment to Quichua ministry.
(*photo: John Maust*)

pressing further. What would it take to get through to the Quichuas?

Ever the optimist, Henry was not going to give up. G. Christian Weiss, director of the mission, paid the Klassens a visit in Colta. Henry broached a request he had been harboring for some time.

"We'd like to make some changes, Dr. Weiss."

"Oh, really? What kind?"

"Well, we're not exactly sure yet."

"Go ahead then, Henry. Don't take this wrong, but we can't do much worse than we've already been doing."

Weiss suggested turning the mission's day school in Colta into a boarding school. Henry and Pat agreed that was a good idea. Missionaries Mary Warkentine and Joyce Benston had started a three-month school on mission property, and the Quichua children seemed excited about it. Roughly twenty-two boys attended. At night eleven girls were learning to read and write. Mary and Joyce were also working on a Quichua grammar with visiting linguist Ellen Ross.

What mission director Weiss did not tell the Klassens, however, was the possibility for an even bigger change: terminating the Quichua work entirely.

Weiss had made his first trip to Ecuador in 1941. Before the trip, he had been particularly concerned about ministry to the head-hunting Jivaro Indians in the Amazon Basin. But seeing the plight of the Quichuas disturbed him even more.

"My impression [of the Quichuas] was that of men and women lying beside the trails in drunken stupor, sometimes with their small children vainly trying to get them on their feet and back to their miserable huts," Weiss remembered later in a *Good News Broadcaster* article.

"Drunken brawls and bloody fights were common. The few missionaries among them often did their best to patch up severe wounds the Indians had inflicted upon one another with machetes."

During that first trip, Weiss met with Woodward and two other single women missionaries among the Quichuas. They informed him there were no converts. When he re-

51

turned again to Chimborazo in 1945, there were still no converts. Another visit in 1954 showed the situation essentially the same. All that being considered, he and other mission leaders questioned whether the work should continue.

## A question of stewardship

In 1954 Weiss stepped down as GMU director, and Don Shidler assumed the post. Now it was Shidler who faced the decision about the future of Quichua mission outreach.

"I don't think it's good stewardship of missions dollars to keep pouring them into the Quichua work," a mission executive told Shidler.

"Besides, other areas of the country seem more open to the gospel," the man added. "You've got a limited number of workers. Place them where they will make the biggest impact."

But Shidler wondered how the mission could merely abandon a work to which Julia Woodward and other missionaries had given their lives? Was *that* good stewardship?

Shidler made two visits to the Quichua work in several years' time. "Henry, you just keep at it," Shidler told Klassen, as encouraging as he had been at Briercrest.

"We've finally got the Quichua New Testament," Henry added. Mrs. Woodward's long-awaited translation had just made it to the field on July 3, 1954.

"And I like what the ladies are doing in the boarding school," said Shidler. "Once those kids start learning to read they'll be using the Bible. I'm sure the Lord is going to do something here yet."

Shidler went away from Colta convinced in his own mind that the Quichua work must go on. If anything, he wanted to send *more* missionaries there. If the mission intended to stay, it should give the work everything and everybody it could spare.

## Making some changes

Henry kept working. He made some of those changes he

had thought about. The first was changing Sunday worship to the afternoon.

"I guess that shows how North American we are," he told Pat, "having church at 11:00 a.m." That would have been OK, except the village emptied completely on Sunday mornings when the Quichuas went to the market in nearby Cajabamba. The Klassens instead started holding services at 4:00 p.m. when the train passed through. Maybe they could attract some of the people who gathered then.

Sometimes four, six or even eight people came to the services, and the Klassens felt encouraged. Then came their first experience in Colta with Carnival, the weeklong feast.

Watching the local Quichuas who were feasting, singing and dancing on the roads, Henry felt sick when he spotted every one of the people he had thought were good potential believers.

Adding insult to injury, men on horseback rode past the mission station shouting, "These foreigners! They don't even believe in the Virgin. Why have those foreign devils come here? Why don't they go home?"

Immediately, Klassen thought to himself, "Yeah, what are we doing in another country? We aren't accomplishing anything down here. We have a good message, but it doesn't mean anything to them."

Usually the eternal optimist, Klassen that night felt as low as he had ever felt. He also nursed a deep anger against the men who had insulted him, and he felt like washing his hands of them.

But slowly the resentment and depression ebbed away. The missionary realized he had been trying to justify himself, and he sensed a gentle reproach from the Lord. He had come to give these people the gospel, not reject them.

So Henry renewed his desire to befriend and evangelize the Quichuas. He had the message they needed—if only he could communicate it.

**Functional substitute**

As a way to deepen the faith of the handful of Quichua

53

believers, the missionaries decided to start weeklong Bible institutes in Colta. They drove to the mission stations in Pulucate and Caliata and brought the few evangelicals or sympathizers from each place. It felt good when the entire group numbered a dozen.

After one such institute, the missionaries determined that four young people were ready for baptism. These Quichuas had made professions of faith, and they seemed committed.

As the sun peaked over the mountains on Easter Sunday, a small group of missionaries and Quichuas walked down to Lake Colta. Henry baptized them, and then everyone went back to the Klassens' living room for the Lord's Supper.

"Imagine! 1955 and today was the first ever Quichua baptism," Pat said.

"It's sure the highlight of my short missionary career," Henry said. "I hope those young people stick. We'll really need to support them."

The local priest had spread the warning that the evangelical baptisms would destroy the lake's fish and plant life. The evangelical heretics had polluted the water, he said. Since so many local Quichuas depended on the lake reeds for animal feed and for making mats, the reports upset them and they scorned the young converts.

So far in Colta, religious opposition had stayed at a minimum. Henry suspected that because there were so few evangelicals, the religious establishment had not yet felt threatened. The baptisms might change that.

If opposition did come, it was important the evangelicals stand together. That made it especially significant that three men in Colta—Manuel Bueno, Nicolás Lamar and Manuel Bahua Cajas—accepted the Lord. They were respected men in the community. They, if anyone, might be able to convince others to stand with them for Jesus.

These same three converts favored the idea of holding a church conference during Carnival. Should not something positive be offered in place of the fiestas? Otherwise, they and others might be tempted or forced back into the old drinking sprees.

54

So in the mid-1950s the missionaries organized the first-ever church conference. The Quichua believers spent Carnival at the Colta station. They sang gospel songs, prayed, studied the Bible and enjoyed each other's company. Unbeknownst to the missionaries, the three Quichua leaders felt tempted to sneak out at night to watch the fiestas. But they resisted the temptation.

"You see, you can have a good time without going to the fiestas." the missionaries said. And everyone seemed to agree. More conferences were planned for the future.

**Exciting report**

Exciting reports came from missionary Dora Regier, a six-foot-tall Midwesterner with the pioneering spirit of Julia Woodward. Dora had started the mission station in Pulucate in 1950.

"We're meeting every day with a family in the village of El Troje," she said.

Four brothers, leaders in the community, had publicly accepted the Lord.

"This may be the breakthrough we've been waiting for," said one of the missionaries. Others voiced caution. Quichuas had accepted the gospel before—only to fall away.

55

# SOMETHING BETTER

For years, old *Señor* Mullo in the village of El Troje had told each of his four sons, "There has to be a better way of life for the Quichuas."

His village, located southwest of Caliata, consisted of homes resting on either side of a beautiful narrow valley that was too small for the nearby hacienda to become especially wealthy or powerful. He was a so-called free Indian—one not tied to a Spanish landlord. So *Señor* Mullo had the freedom to dream of a better day for his family and people.

He was a weaver. Like most Quichua men of his day, he made the ponchos, skirts, muslin pants and other simple clothing for family members. *Señor* Mullo worked hard to feed his wife and four sons, and he insisted that his sons be honest in all their dealings.

Mullo told his sons, "Something is wrong with the feasts, but I don't know exactly what it is."

Why should I spend a year's wages or more on food and drink on a religious fiesta? he thought. Sponsoring a religious fiesta was supposed to bring great blessing. But he and everyone else wound up working that much harder in a vain attempt to recuperate the money they had lost.

The people from El Troje and nearby communities poured thousands of Eucadorian *sucres* into the nearby town of Columbe, a proverbial den of iniquity. Besides its big Catholic church, large market and many official offices, the town was glutted with saloons and houses of prostitution. Not surprisingly, it also had a large graveyard.

Quichuas from all the large surrounding communities converged on Columbe for their feast days, weddings and funerals. It was a place to file grievances and find money lenders.

Because most of the outlying villages did not have a Catholic church, the Quichuas also went to Columbe for confession and mass. Afterward, they patronized the money-hungry liquor merchants and kept on drinking on the way home. Sometimes they slept off their drunkenness alongside the road, or they stopped at homes of friends and relatives and kept right on drinking. Meanwhile, their children back home went hungry or fended for themselves.

Mostly because of community pressure, *Señor* Mullo went along with the fiestas and fulfilled his obligations. Anyone who did not was called "a dog." Besides, if he rejected the system, what would he replace it with? There had to be something better, but what?

### Like father, like son

Matías, the third of four sons, shared his father's way of looking beneath the surface of things. He too desired a better life. Thirsty for knowledge, Matías could neither read nor write. Inquisitive about spiritual things, he did not understand the priest's teachings regarding judgment and rituals.

As a boy, Matías heard stories from his elders about the Bible. There were stories about Noah and the flood, Adam and Eve and a feared last judgment, for instance. But these were mixed with Quichua legends, and Matías really did not know what he believed.

Over the years, people in his village had either seen or heard about the white-skinned missionary, Julia Woodward. Religious leaders called her and other missionaries Protestant "devils," "heretics," or worse.

Matías did not know the truth of these charges, but he had no particular reason to investigate them. Now if these

57

missionaries could do something for him, say, help him learn to read and write, they would be worth knowing.

A GMU missionary, Elma Voth, had made initial contact with the people of El Troje. Traveling cross-country on a return trip to the mission station in Pulucate, Elma and Ecuadorian co-worker Esther Palma had stumbled across the valley almost by accident, and they decided to visit some homes.

The women had some medicines and simple remedies. When the Quichas found out, they started shouting across the fields that women had come to treat their sick. Afterward, the GMU missionaries in Pulucate started making trips about once a week with medicines to El Troje.

With little medical training, the missionaries did what they could to treat the Quichuas and make friends for the gospel. While the illnesses were not overly serious—eye and ear infections, toothaches, running sores and skin diseases—they made life miserable for the Quichuas.

**It started with a cow**

Soon everyone in El Troje was surprised to hear that the Protestant missionaries were regularly visiting the home of Juan Naula—known for throwing the "best" fiestas in the village. Juan Naula with the Protestant missionaries in his home?

Naula's wife, Transita, had been tugging an ornery bull across the Pan American Highway, when a passing car startled the animal. It bucked and came down hard on one of Transita's bare feet. She suffered for days when the nasty wound got infected and would not heal. Visitors to her home felt certain she would die.

Almost in desperation, Juan remembered the missionaries in nearby Pulucate. He walked there to see if they would come treat his wife. And he returned home content, because Dora Regier and Elma Voth promised they would go to El Troje the following day if he would provide them a horse for the trip.

The missionaries started to visit the Naula home every

day. As they treated her foot and changed the bandage, they also told the family about Christ. They took along a hand-cranked Victrola record player and recordings of hymns and Scripture readings, which fascinated the six Naula children.

Transita's foot began healing well, but Juan Naula did not want the missionaries to stop coming. He practically begged them to teach his six children to read and write. Almost no one was literate in the village, and the classes would be a way for his children to get ahead in life.

Seeing Naula's request as an open door for the gospel into El Troje, the missionaries happily accepted his request. They knew about the evangelistic potential of schools, having run one for the past several years at the mission station in Pulucate.

The missionaries started holding classes twice a week on the front porch of the Naulas' mud hut. News of the classes spread, and other children began attending. A cousin of the Naula children, José Juan, went to the classes even though his father forbade him.

"If you go to school, you'll start to become lazy like the *cholos*. You won't want to work in the fields," the father said.

José Juan's mother had more progressive ideas, however. She sent the boy on errands to the uncle's home when she knew the classes were being held.

During this time, GMU missionary doctor Donald Dilworth started making regular medical visits to El Troje. And the women continued with reading and Bible classes.

## Search for truth

Matías Mullo knew of fellow Quichuas over the years who outwardly followed the missionaries' teaching. But he held the opinion that these people had been out for what they could get—medical care, literature, and maybe even gifts of clothing, food or a little prestige.

As far as Matías was concerned, he did not need all the *things* the missionaries might have to offer. But he did want to know the truth about the missionaries' teachings and the Bible. He also wanted them to teach him to read so he could study for himself.

One day Matías decided to visit the missionaries when they came to El Troje. He took along a gift of fresh milk, hoping it would win their favor and confidence. And he asked lots of questions. Matías also began attending the literacy classes in El Troje. Later he attended the missionaries' school in Pulucate, so that in three months' time, he had reached the second grade.

Matías also managed to buy one of the Quichua New Testaments. And he often read late into the night after his wife was asleep. Married now for three years, he only stopped reading to calm the baby if it started crying.

For Matías, the Bible was like a forbidden fruit. The priests often talked about the Bible, but very few Quichuas had actually read one. Nevertheless, Matías could not understand much of what he was reading.

**Profession of faith**

During these days, the missionaries planned a daily vacation Bible school for the children in El Troje. Night meetings were programed for everyone. GMU missionary Margaret McGivney and Lydia Cortéz, a Spanish Bible school student, organized the Bible school. They had planned to hold the meetings outside in a large yard, but heavy rains forced them onto a small porch.

Quichuas climbed up the steep muddy hill to the meetings. The women taught some Christian hymns, and Quichua attenders responded enthusiastically, singing about an hour before each evening meeting. McGivney gave flannelgraph lessons in her halting Quichua, and Lydia delivered an evangelistic message in Spanish.

Matías went to one of those meetings, and he objected when the speaker said, "Anyone who believes has the power to become a son of God."

"There must be more to it than that," Matías challenged. "Everyone around here believes in God."

"You're right, Matías," the speaker said. "There is more to it than that. True faith changes a person's heart and life." Matías was shown the Scripture saying that even the demons believe in the existence of God. He was directed to other Bible verses, and suddenly the message clicked. Joy surged into Matías, because now he finally understood what salvation meant. That night he prayed for Jesus to forgive his sins and to make him the kind of new person the missionaries talked about.

Matías immediately shared his spiritual experience with his three brothers. They remained skeptical. Maybe this was just another of their enthusiastic brother's new ideas. But Matías argued and persuaded. His brothers also went to the evening meetings, and within a week's time all four had decided to commit their lives to Christ.

It was especially important that José Mullo decided to accept the missionaries' teaching, because as the oldest brother he had a major say in family matters.

### "My eyes are closed"

Though his brothers had chosen to follow Christ, Matías could not convince his wife, Mercedes.

"My eyes are closed," Mercedes would say, as her husband repeatedly explained the gospel.

Finally, Matías struck a deal with his wife. "You go to mass on Sunday," Matías said, "and I'll go hear the missionaries. When we get home, we'll compare what we learned."

Because Mercedes did not understand the Catholic services, the little review sessions became monologues for Matías, who repreached the message he had heard that day. Before long, Mercedes also became a Christian.

As he walked to the market with people from his community, Matías preached Christ. When he visited relatives, he witnessed about Christ. And when he approached his neighbors, the enthusiastic young Christian presented the gospel. Sometimes the spiritual discussions in neighbors' homes lasted all night.

## Increased opposition

The handful of evangelicals in El Troje met increasing opposition in the village. It seemed to Matías that people were not rejecting the gospel as such; rather, fellow Quichuas opposed the evangelicals out of fear of the religious and Spanish authorities. Also, people did not want to break with centuries-old superstitions and customs.

The community really got upset, however, when the evangelicals acted upon their new faith by making drastic changes in their lifestyles.

The Mullo brothers infuriated the community leaders when they stopped serving them the corn liquor *chicha*. (The community leaders did not get paid for organizing the local feast days and community work projects, so they traditionally demanded and received free *chicha* from the neighbors as their rightful fringe benefit.)

The Mullo brothers also refused to pay their assessment for the annual mass in El Troje, which meant there was not enough money in the church budget. In retaliation, a local merchant refused to sell them salt.

When the brothers did not take part in one of the community work projects to whitewash the Catholic chapel, the villagers tried to keep them from using the local water well. (Whenever a Quichua community organized a *minga*, or work project, every able-bodied man was expected to take part. Not doing so meant a fine or punishment.)

As another expression of his new faith, Matías would not carry the image of a saint through the fields when the crops needed rain or protection against hail. Neither would he nor his brothers leave food offerings for Mother Earth or the spirits. So when the crops suffered, angry community leaders blamed the evangelicals.

The Mullo brothers and other evangelicals increasingly faced physical and verbal abuse. Sometimes the Mullo brothers had to walk home through the fields, because assailants were watching for them on the roads.

The priest in Columbe had been informed about the mis-

62

sionaries' visits to El Troje. He was furious the community had allowed in "those daughters of the devil." Juan Naula learned the priest had publicly branded him a "heretic" for allowing missionaries in his home. The priest urged El Troje leaders to burn or drive out the missionaries and evangelicals.

Fear of the priests and the unknown sparked increasing persecution of the evangelicals. People stole animals from the Naulas and Mullos and tried to destroy their crops.

"How are we going to live if this keeps up?" Mercedes asked Matías one day. "The Lord has provided us with enough to eat, but what are we going to do if this keeps up?"

Matías nodded sympathetically. He did not know what would happen either. But as far as he was concerned, he had found the better way of life his father once talked about. If he and the other evangelicals had to pay for their decision, then so be it.

"We're not only living for this life," he said to Mercedes. "We're living for eternal life. And if our souls are saved, what they might do to our bodies is only secondary."

# FIGHTING AGAINST JESUS

Henry Klassen pushed the gas pedal toward the floor. His jeep bounced crazily on the cobble-stoned Pan American Highway, and the windows jiggled so loudly he could barely think. He had to get to El Troje as quickly as possible.

If it were true that a drunken mob had surrounded the tiny church in El Troje, he hated to think what might have happened to Dora and the believers.

This was not the first time Dora had gotten into a tight spot. When she had started the mission station in Pulucate, mobs moved towards her house to burn her out two days in a row. Each time, however, heavy rains sent them home, and the attackers began to sense they were fighting against God, not men, and they let her alone.

Actually, Henry worried more about the Quichua believers than Dora. Dora was tough. She had been threatened before. As to the Quichua believers, so young in their faith, he was not sure. So far, at least, they had shown remarkable strength as persecution against them grew steadily. It hit a peak when the priest in Columbe issued his El Troje parishioners an ultimatum:

"There will be no more administration of the sacraments as long as the evangelicals are permitted here."

That meant no more baptisms, burials, or weddings...and real problems for the Quichuas. For instance, Quichua parents generally could not get birth certificates for their babies if they did not see to it that the babies received Catholic infant baptism.

People began to suspect maybe it *hadn't* rained because the evangelicals refused to carry the idol of the saint through the field. And who were the evangelicals to go against the fiestas? Quichuas had always observed the feasts!

The opposition started getting more physical. El Troje evangelicals began going to the Colta medical clinic for treatment of their cuts and bruises. Still, they wanted the missionaries to come and teach the Bible.

Klassen remembered an experience during his first furlough in 1957, when an uncle asked, "Henry, what kind of church problems do you have among the Quichuas?"

"We don't have any," Henry replied.

"That's amazing," said the uncle. "Tell me. What's your secret?"

"That's easy," said Henry. "We don't have a church."

But now Klassen's statement no longer held true. A year later in 1958, the believers in El Troje built the first-ever Quichua evangelical church. It was cause for great joy among the Quichuas and the missionaries, but the new church seemed to provoke a new wave of opposition.

Henry had advised the El Troje believers, as well as Dora, not to take unnecessary risks. But now it appeared the opposers wanted to quash the evangelicals once and for all.

**Men taken prisoner**

Henry braked where the trail left the highway toward El Troje. He could see a mob coming toward him. There was Dora, standing a head taller than the Quichuas surrounding her. Henry also recognized the commissary, or police chief, from Columbe who would have jurisdiction over matters in the tiny surrounding villages such as El Troje.

"Oh, am I glad to see you," Dora said, when the group reached his jeep. She was flustered but unhurt.

65

"I'll take over, Dora. Get into my jeep." Dora happily complied with Henry's order. Meanwhile, he turned toward the commissary. It appeared that a number of the young believers, including some of the Mullo brothers, had been taken prisoner.

"What's the problem here?" Henry asked, trying to sound as authoritative as possible. He presented himself as chairman of his mission's work among the Quichuas.

"I had to rescue the *Señorita*," the commissary said, surprised to see Henry there.

"I believe there must be more involved than that," Henry said, not batting an eye.

"There has not been any rain for a long time, and the people are blaming you evangelicals for it," piped a Columbe man who had accompanied the police chief. "God is punishing them for having let you into El Troje." He then turned toward the crowd. "Isn't that right?"

Hardly anyone responded.

"These people don't believe that, and I don't either," Henry said.

The police chief interrupted. He was taking six evangelicals to prison for having invited in the missionaries, he said, and he was doing it for their own protection.

"Then I think it would only be fair that you take six from the other side to jail, also," Henry argued.

After more debate, the commissary said, "We'll go to the courthouse and see what can be done."

The group arrived at the courthouse, but nothing happened until the priest arrived. Henry thought that seemed peculiar. Then someone whispered that the police chief and priest were brothers. He knew then that things were going to get worse, not better.

The priest questioned the prisoners, several of them mere boys. They gave him sound, biblical answers.

"Why do you bother us?" the priest asked, turning to Henry. "We all believe in God here. Why don't you stay in the United States where there are atheists and teach *them* about God?"

Trying to remain calm, Klassen pointed out that Ecuador's constitution promised religious freedom. The missionaries had gone into El Troje upon the invitation of the people, Klassen said. He was sorry problems had come up, but the prisoners should be released.

The police chief and priest then conferred, and finally the commissary said the believers must stay in jail. At that point, Henry decided there was nothing more he could do by arguing further, so he took Dora back to Pulucate, where he had left his family and a married couple visiting from Canada.

Over a late lunch, Dora explained what had happened. "When the commissary arrived, he asked all the people in favor of the evangelicals to line up along the church wall," she said.

"Did many of them do it?"

"I was amazed, because more people stood against the wall than had ever before identified with the evangelicals," she said. "The whole situation almost reminded me of a firing squad."

"Those people had courage," said Henry.

After lunch, he and his Canadian friend drove into Columbe. They were going to make sure the young men were getting fair treatment, and he wanted to encourage them.

Henry and Jake poked their heads in front of the basement window below the courthouse. Was that singing they heard? Gospel songs in Quichua?

"Hello, *don Enrique*," called one, spotting the missionary through the window.

"How are you fellows making out?"

"We're having a nice time," said another. "Back home we don't usually have this much time for singing. But here we've got lots of time."

"I guess we don't need to encourage *them*," Henry said, as much to himself as to his friend, Jake. These young believers reminded him of Paul and Silas in Philippi.

Henry called down to the group, saying the next day, Monday, he would seek their release from the provincial authorities in Riobamba. He could not do anything before then, because on Sunday all public offices were closed.

As Henry and Jake prepared to leave town, a group of local women shouted threats and curses.

"We're going to pour gas on you and send you out in ashes if you ever come back," was one Henry understood.

"What did they say?" asked Jake, who did not speak Spanish.

"They said we'd better not come back here," Henry said, softening his translation. Jake lived only seven miles from Henry's mother, and she would get worried if Jake told her the literal version.

## Believers released

The next day Henry brought an authority from Riobamba. The official immediately had the prisoners released, and he scolded the Columbe police chief for having violated their constitutional freedoms.

The Troje believers returned home with fire in their eyes. They started gathering nightly for prayer meetings in each other's adobe homes. They needed to stick together, because persecution against them continued.

One of the missionaries, Dr. Dilworth, went into the village during the feasting and was mobbed by a crowd of drunks. They beat him and hauled him to the ground. The doctor had a gun with him, and in desperation he fired low into the crowd. He hit a man in the leg, and the drunken mob stopped beating him. Some believers were then able to rescue the doctor. It so happened that the badly beaten missionary and the wounded Quichua spent the night in adjacent rooms in the same Riobamba medical clinic.

The unfortunate incident reinforced in everyone's minds that for the time being the missionaries should stay out of El Troje. Their presence would further irritate the situation and possibly endanger the believers even more.

It was hard for the missionaries to stay away, since they knew their brothers and sisters in Christ faced difficult times. But matters would have to be entrusted to the Lord. God would have to protect his church in El Troje.

## "Fighting against the one I serve"

One day friends brought Matías Mullo to the Colta clinic. His shoulder hung limp. Cuts and bruises marked his face and body. Despite his injuries, Matías looked in good spirits and he was praising God for his deliverance.

Matías explained that he was going to work in his field when a group of men had circled him. "Now we're going to drink blood," one of them growled. "We'll teach you for being against our feasts." They attacked Matías with clubs and took away the only thing he might have used as a weapon—his hoe. The drunken men ripped Matías's clothes off in the struggle. Whirling and grappling, the group moved toward the edge of a ravine. Miraculously, Matías kept on his feet. If he had fallen to the ground, they would have torn at him like wolves.

Suddenly Matías found himself at the edge of a deep ravine, and the mob pushed him off. Matías fell onto a cactus bed, and the men tossed heavy clods of earth on top of him.

Matías looked thirty feet up to the men, his face bleeding, and said, "You're not really fighting me. You're fighting against the one I serve, Jesus Christ."

"You're not of Christ. You're the devil."

"Go ahead and kill me," Matías said. "My family will go right on believing."

Somehow, Matías crawled away. When the men attacked him again on his way home, his brothers and some neighbors drove them off. Only after Matías lay safely inside his house did he realize the full extent of what had happened. He had fallen onto wicked, inch-long thorns, but not one had punctured him. The cactus had felt as soft as a sponge.

"It's a miracle," he told his family. "God really does protect us." His persecutors, amazed that Matías had survived, accused him of having a demon.

More stories like this one convinced the missionaries that at least in El Troje, Quichua believers would stand firm.

# GEARING UP IN COLTA

With the missionaries temporarily not going into El Troje, they turned their attention to the station in Colta. Several new projects had just gotten started, and more personnel had arrived.

Following two years in another ministry in Quito, the capital city, Henry Klassen in 1961 returned to full-time Quichua work in Chimborazo. The boarding school at Colta had extended its school year to nine months, and the mission wanted Henry to oversee construction of an additional school building as the number of students kept growing.

Missionary teacher Mary Warkentine had noticed that new children at the school typically balked at hard tasks with a simple, *"No puedo,"* "I can't." So Mary and the other teachers told the students to eliminate that phrase from their vocabularies.

Once the Quichuas saw that they could learn to do new things, their attitude changed 100 percent and their *"no puedo"* was replaced by "teach me."

Not only did the students study the basics—reading, writing and arithmetic—they also learned about personal hygiene and how to play musical instruments and bake bread.

"They want to learn everything we can give them," Mary said, though not complaining. She did not know how to play the accordion herself. But because of the Quichuas' in-

70

terest in music and because accordions would be useful in worship services, Mary began giving accordion classes from a how-to manual. Before long, several Quichuas were playing the instrument like old pros.

The mission had obtained government accreditation for its Atahualpa School. An Ecuadorian taught the reading, writing and arithmetic, and the missionaries taught Bible classes for half an hour after every regular school day. They also started work projects that would help the students pay their tuition.

The students, who ranged from small children to adults, learned to sew and embroider. They also began making peanut butter and grated coconut. Their products earned a reputation for quality and sold quickly in nearby markets. Not only did the projects provide income, the students learned simple vocational skills that would last them a lifetime.

### Lesson in foot-washing

New missionary Roberta Hostetter took charge of the children's medical care. Since nearly all the students went barefoot to school, Roberta began at "ground level." Each morning before classes, she washed and treated the children's cut and infected feet. Spanish medical officials from nearby Riobamba, visiting the school one day, stood open-mouthed at the sight of a white woman washing Indians' feet.

The missionaries had noticed that many children did not want to take off their ponchos, even on warm days and inside the classroom. One day Roberta found out why when she asked a boy to remove his poncho. He did so with great embarrassment, revealing a bare bottom and tattered pants with the seat entirely worn out. After that experience, Roberta and the other missionaries set to work mending children's clothes or making new ones.

Some children made Christian commitments at the school. And they returned home on weekends as little missionaries—singing choruses and telling Bible stories they had learned during the previous week.

Meanwhile, on the other side of Majipamba, the mission bought property for a clinic and a hospital. Missionary doctor Donald Dilworth spearheaded this medical project, which quickly attracted large numbers of Quichuas tired of being mistreated or ignored by the Spanish physicians.

In his journal, Henry Klassen recorded that in 1961 some 3,452 patients received treatment at the mission clinic and hospital. This "presented opportunity to give the Gospel message to the patients and their families who came with them."

**Radio project**

One day Dr. Dilworth was hiking across the mountains between the Colta and Caliata mission stations, and he stopped for a rest. For curiosity's sake, he started counting Quichua houses on the surrounding hillsides.

He reasoned within himself that if he visited each home for fifteen minutes, working an eight-hour day, it would take two full years to visit each one of those houses only once.

Then it dawned upon him. The answer was radio! Radio would take the missionaries immediately into homes and villages which otherwise might not hear the gospel for years. Dilworth shared his idea with the other missionaries and got approval from the mission for a radio project.

The problem was getting a goverment permit. Dilworth brought up the matter with Frederico Martínez of the big *Tres Monjas* hacienda in Colta, who had been elected governor of Chimborazo Province. The two had become friends when Dilworth taught the man how to hunt and fish. When Martínez's workers stole some sheep from Colta believer Manuel Bahua Cajas, Dilworth asked Martínez to return the sheep, and he did.

Later, Martínez arranged for the doctor to sit across the table from Ecuadorian President Ibarra at a banquet in Riobamba. Dilworth had just enough of a conversation with the president to mention the radio station permit.

"Whatever it is they want, you be sure they get it," Ibarra told his secretary.

The papers came through with the stipulation that the station be on the air within eighty-nine days. Dilworth hurriedly raised funds for the radio project and, with technical help from World Radio HCJB in Quito, radio station HCUE-5 was operating in eighty-eight days out of a building next to the Colta clinic.

Almost immediately, the five-watt station began proving itself an effective communications tool among the Quichuas.

The mission sold sixty transistor radios, pretuned to the new station's frequency. These radios found their way into thirteen different Quichua communities and created surprising interest among listeners. It was not unusual to see twenty or thirty people crowded around one radio.

Henry Klassen heard a blaring noise one day. He looked outside to see a man, obviously drunk, carrying a radio. As Klassen listened more closely, he recognized gospel preaching and music from the Quichua radio station. Out of curiosity, the missionary decided to approach the man.

"Excuse me, may I ask you a question?"

"What do you want to know?" said the man, eyeing the foreigner suspiciously.

"I assume you're not an evangelical, so I'm just wondering why you're listening to the gospel on the radio."

"Because it speaks my language, that's why," the man retorted, proceeding on his way.

Quichua preachers began teaching the Bible to illiterate listeners. A greetings program, allowing the few Quichua evangelicals to go to the station to salute their non-Christian friends and family members, quickly attracted interest. Unsuspecting listeners, hearing their names over the radio, seemed to pay greater attention to the gospel.

For some Quichuas, the radios seemed to represent some kind of supernatural power. A man who had lost his cat asked Klassen to consult the radio about where to find it.

Between its school, radio station and hospital, the mission needed plenty of personnel to keep things going. So

73

more workers were added. The missionary force among the Quichuas reached almost twenty in the early 1960s. Having an abundance of workers led to inevitable interpersonal conflicts. But the workers managed to maintain their unity of purpose.

With so many workers and ministries moving into place, the timing seemed ripe for the long-awaited spiritual breakthrough among the Quichuas.

# SHOWDOWN IN SAN ANTONIO

The village of San Antonio, just across the lake from the mission station in Colta, looked like a place out of America's Old West. A dozen saloons lined its dusty streets. Next to liquor, the most profitable business in town belonged to the coffin-maker.

San Antonio looked like the last place for a gospel breakthrough. And Pablo Suqui, who lived there, seemed the least likely candidate for Christian conversion.

One day Pablo decided to go the Colta mission clinic for tuberculosis treatments. He had been forced to spend his life's savings on doctors in Riobamba, Guayaquil and Quito, who treated him without success. So Pablo, who generally despised the evangelicals, figured he did not have anything to lose by going to their clinic in Colta. Besides, it was only about two miles from his home.

Early in the morning Pablo went to the clinic. According to custom, a Quichua employee gave a short evangelistic message to the waiting patients before the clinic opened. Upset by what he was hearing, Pablo began to swear, yell and make so much noise that finally the speaker, Pedro Bahua, asked to have Pablo put outside the gate until devotions ended.

"You're of the devil," Pablo yelled through the gate.

"If you don't want to listen, at least let the others listen," said Bahua.

75

Pablo's treatment required an injection every day for a month, so each morning the situation repeated itself. Pablo would harrass the Bible teacher and then be banished outside until the message finished.

But the gate was not soundproof. Pedro Bahua began to observe that Pablo was actually listening. One day, to the surprise of everyone, Pablo asked to accept Jesus as his personal Savior. Missionaries and Quichuas alike wondered if he was really serious. They found out how serious Pablo was when he began dragging friends and relatives to the clinic to hear the gospel.

Word came from San Antonio that Pablo had rigged up a loudspeaker to his radio at home. Quichua preaching from radio station HCUE-5 began blasting throughout the village. Irate neighbors threatened to burn Pablo's house if he did not quit. Pablo did disconnect the speaker, but he kept right on witnessing with the exuberance that once characterized his opposition to the gospel.

The missionaries had known of evangelical sympathizers in San Antonio, a community known for its Quichua merchants who sold weavings and other goods throughout Ecuador and in other South American countries. But they had never met any committed believers in the village until Pablo.

For years, Dr. Dilworth could not even get into San Antonio with medical clinics. As far as he could tell, the village was part of an old matriarchal group, controlled by one old woman.

But now, a short time after Pablo Suqui's conversion, the missionaries began hearing reports of Quichuas making decisions to follow Christ.

"There are twenty-two families in San Antonio who have accepted the Lord," Pablo told Klassen one day.

"Twenty-two *persons* or twenty-two *families*?" Klassen wanted to know.

"Twenty-two families," Pablo repeated.

"How can families accept the Lord?"

"The Bible says to believe on the Lord and you and your house will be saved," said Pablo.

76

"Well, yes, but..." Klassen stopped. The idea of families converting did not fit into his frame of spiritual reference.

"That's the way we Quichuas do it," Pablo explained. "Usually the head of the family makes a decision, and then after he explains it to the others, and they make the same decision with him."

## Can families accept the Lord?

Could it be possible? Could a whole family make a profession of faith? The idea confused and fascinated the missionaries, who generally saw salvation as a personal decision and not a group one. Yet after decades of spiritual drought in Chimborazo, here were not a handful of converts, but twemty-two *families* wanting to join the evangelical church.

The missionaries remembered how important it had been in El Troje that the four Mullo brothers—influential in their community—publicly profess their faith. Indeed, nearly all of their immediate family members had also accepted the Lord. What would happen if this kind of family movement spread to other Quichua communities?

Apparently, the saloonkeepers in San Antonio were asking the same kinds of questions. They could foresee their liquor profits literally going down the drain if the whole town converted to teetotaling evangelicalism. Also, Catholic leaders feared losing an entire flock. For the time being, the community adopted a wait-and-see attitude.

Then the San Antonio evangelicals announced their desire for public baptism, and they asked the missionaries to conduct a baptismal service on the San Antonio side of the lake.

This did not seem prudent to the missionaries, remembering the opposition provoked by the first baptism in Colta. Henry Klassen advised, "Why don't you have the service on our side of the lake, where people are more sympathetic?"

"No, we think it will be all right," they said. "It will be a witness to the nonbelievers."

77

The day before the scheduled baptism, the enthusiastic San Antonio converts waded into the shallow lake to hollow out a place deep enough for the baptism. Meanwhile, Carnival feasting was in full swing, and a drunken mob gathered at the shore. They warned that evangelical baptisms were forbidden in San Antonio, but the believers shrugged off their threats. Hearing about this confrontation, the missionaries again wondered about the wisdom of going through with the baptism.

Late that night, Pat Klassen awakened to a sharp tapping on the bedroom window. She turned on the light and saw it was 4:00 a.m. Henry woke up also, and the couple peered through the window.

"Wake up. Wake up. Our brothers from San Antonio have been attacked by a mob, and they need help!"

It was Manuel Bueno, Quichua church leader from Colta. The Klassens hurriedly threw on their clothes and opened the door to Manuel and a group of cut and bruised San Antonio believers.

"What happened to you?" the missionaries exclaimed.

Everyone spoke at once. The evangelicals had been meeting that night in someone's home. A mob had approached, and for two hours drunken feast-goers pelted the house with rocks and bricks. Windows were broken, and most of the clay tiles on the roof had given way and fallen on top of the believers, who huddled in the dark until after midnight when it would be safer to escape.

The believers guessed the canteen owners had gotten the people drunk—even giving them free liquor—and then worked them up against the evangelicals with the same old rumors: missionaries eat people's flesh, evangelicals are devils and an evangelical baptism will destroy the lake. The saloon keepers wanted to stop anyone who would hurt their lucrative trade, and some twenty-two evangelical families were "boycotting" the Carnival feasting.

The injured San Antonio believers received treatment at the clinic, and then spent the night at the boarding school and in Colta believers' homes.

Early the next morning, the missionary men decided to

go to the authorities in Riobamba to request help for the San Antonio believers.

"You just don't understand the Indians," said the authority, not convinced the turmoil in San Antonio was anything out of the ordinary. "But, all right, I'll go with you to talk with the leaders in San Antonio."

Henry drove the official and two policemen into the village where they were met by an angry mob numbering at least 500. Henry did not like the looks of things, and neither did Pat, worried about her husband's safety. She sighted her husband through the scope of a rifle—the closest thing at home to binoculars.

Henry kept his jeep running while the official confidently got out and walked into the crowd. The missionary could see people wildly gesticulating, and it looked like the man from Riobamba was in trouble.

Even the policemen feared for their lives. "You'd better come back or we're leaving!" they yelled.

The official unceremoniously hustled back to the waiting vehicle, and Klassen accelerated under a cloud of rocks, sticks and mud clods.

Now the official conceded the need for a stronger show of force. He sent a truckload of soldiers, but even they failed to disperse the mob.

The missionaries decided to again petition for help in Riobamba, this time to the provincial governor.

Unknown to them, however, the drunken mob in San Antonio was planning an attack on the missionaries. Only the missionary wives remained in Majipamba—Pat Klassen, Beverly Adkisson, Virginia Haynes and little daughter Debra.

The women held their breath as a mob of 600 or 700 headed around the edge of the lake toward the mission station. Then, miraculously, the mob fell back. The group started forward, and again stopped, as if confused.

Meanwhile, in Riobamba, the governor promised to send fifty soldiers to San Antonio. But he requested permission for the soldiers to stay overnight at the mission station, so they could leave before dawn the following morning to round up the main troublemakers. Also, the governor asked that a few San Antonio evangelicals go along to identify the ringleaders.

Back in Colta, Klassen explained the situation to the San Antonio believers—generally baffled that the government for once seemed to be on their side.

## Soldiers enter San Antonio

The soldiers arrived that night, according to plan, and they slept in the boarding school. Meanwhile, the San Antonio believers stayed up most of the night praying and deciding who should accompany the soldiers in the morning. A group of believers from Majipamba joined them, and new unity and fellowship was established that night between believers from the two villages.

As a witness to the soldiers, the Quichuas decided to serve them a breakfast of coffee and bread rolls. Then at 4:00 a.m. the convoy of soldiers and about a dozen San Antonians pulled out. Watching them leave, missionaries and Quichuas prayed for a peaceful quick resolution of the problem.

Evidently their prayers were heard, because in little more than an hour the soldiers returned with about fifteen prisoners, now looking as meek as kittens. The troublemakers were taken next to Riobamba, where they lost whatever fight they had left.

It was several days before the San Antonio believers felt it safe to return home. When they did return, many found their water wells contaminated—people had thrown dead dogs into some of them. Homes were damaged, fields untended and animals unfed.

Still, the believers did not seek revenge against their persecutors. Their forgiving attitude impressed the skeptics, who sensed maybe there was something different about this new teaching. Some of the persecutors even decided to follow Jesus.

Luis Asitimbay had been one of the most violent opponents of the evangelicals in San Antonio. But after his conversion, he said, "No matter what happens, I want others to understand what I didn't at first.

"I want to preach even if somebody throws stones at me—just as I used to throw stones at believers. I want to know what it feels like to be on the other end."

# 12

# WINDS OF CHANGE

After the mini-people movement in San Antonio, small spiritual breakthroughs popped out like delicate flowers on the Andean hillsides.

Budding church growth testified to a new movement of God in Chimborazo. But it also bore witness to fresh winds of change gusting across Ecuador in the early 1960s. Powerful political and religious currents were sweeping away longtime obstacles to advance of the gospel, namely, the hacienda system and religious intolerance.

Only about ten years before, when Christian linguist and anthropologist William Reyburn lived in the San Antonio area, "a word from the hacienda owner to the priest was sufficient to clamp a man and his sons into jail indefinitely with subsequent loss of sharecropping rights," he said.

But then came 1964, a year that would radically alter the future of thousands of Quichuas and rural peasants. Ecuador's military government in 1964 adopted an agrarian reform law, intended to break up the big haciendas and give Indians the privilege of buying land for themselves. The law eliminated the system in which Quichuas worked for free on the haciendas in exchange for a tiny family plot for subsistence farming.

There were problems implementing the law in a way that

would truly benefit the Quichuas. Some Quichuas rioted on the haciendas and attempted to seize the land from absentee owners. And some leftist groups agitated villagers, telling Quichuas the land was theirs in the first place, so why should they have to buy it from the whites?

But despite the difficulties, the new legislation gave Quichuas new hope and a sense of their own rights.

For the first time, Quichuas were forced to make decisions affecting the course of their lives. In the process, they became free to consider new options, such as the evangelicals' teachings.

"The Quichuas were never really against the message of the gospel," said Reyburn. "They did not have the freedom to innovate at any level of their lives: social, political, economic, religious. They owed their precarious existence to the owner of the land, the hacienda owner. The latter was always a white man, a right-wing conservative Roman Catholic."

Agrarian reform "significantly affected the lives of many Indians who began to escape the control of the hacienda, as many Indian communities became independent," wrote anthropologist and missionary Rubén "Tito" Paredes.

"The Quichuas were now able to hear the Gospel with fewer obstacles and choose to accept if they wanted to."

**Evangelical association formed**

Land reform had a very practical application for the Quichua believers in Chimborazo.

Salable land through land reform became available in the Colta area in 1966, and Quichua Christians wanted to get some for a church. Several of the leaders and missionary Henry Klassen went to a land reform official in Riobamba, who said there would be no problem. In fact, land for a church would not cost them anything, the man said.

"Do you have a cemetery?" he asked. The Quichuas said no. "Well, why don't you apply for enough land to have a cemetery?"

Everyone thought that was a good idea, since until then

they had been using the little plot alongside Klassen's house.

"How about a soccer field? Do you have a soccer field?" the official continued.

The Quichua leaders did not really think a soccer field was necessary. They had never even played soccer—a white man's game—until recently. But after talking matters over, they decided it would not hurt to get some extra land next to the church if it was all part of the same package and did not cost extra.

The only stipulation was the Quichuas needed to apply for the land through a legally recognized entity. They immediately suggested Gospel Missionary Union.

"Oh, no," said the lawyer. "Foreigners are not allowed to receive land under the agrarian reform law."

For a long time Henry Klassen had wanted the believers to form a legally recognized association. Besides giving the Quichuas greater autonomy in ministry matters, an association would give them badly needed legal standing for defending themselves in cases of persecution.

Necessity became the mother of invention. The Quichua leaders in Colta, who had previously resisted the idea, realized they needed an association.

"But we don't know how to draw up the statutes of an association," they said.

Klassen suggested they use the mission's statutes as a model, and the work began. The Quichuas' application was approved, and in 1966 the believers got not only land for a church, but also their own organization, the Association of Indigenous Evangelicals of Chimborazo (AIECH).

## Catholic reform

About the same time as Ecuadorian land reform, Roman Catholic leaders from around the world gathered for the Second Vatican Council (1962-1965), or Vatican II. The purpose of the council, according to Pope John XXIII, was spiritual renewal and reformation within Roman Catholicism and among its members. As one result of the council,

Latin evangelicals noted a welcome decrease in Roman Catholic/Protestant tensions.

Vatican II documents said Protestants should be considered "separated brethren." Catholics should even be allowed to pray with Protestants. Vatican II also maintained a person's right to religious freedom. The documents declared that "all men are to be immune from coercion on the part of individuals or of social groups and of any human power."

Finally, the Council promoted a return to Scripture: "Easy access to sacred Scripture should be provided for all the Christian faithful." This was especially good news for Latin evangelicals, people of "the Book."

It took awhile for reforms to filter into outlying areas like Ecuador's Chimborazo Province, and religious fanaticism persisted through the 1960s in many of the villages. But Quichuas did begin to experience and observe reforms of different kinds in the Roman Catholic Church.

The activist Archbishop Leonidas Proaño of Riobamba began helping the Quichuas form cooperatives, and he launched a radio station for teaching literacy classes. As the church's contribution to land reform, he reportedly gave away thousands of acres of church land to the Quichuas for development projects.

**Increased mobility**

Increasing numbers of Quichuas began migrating to the big cities for seasonal or short-term work. Many worked in the sugar-cane fields on the coast near Guayaquil or they worked in factories. Often they did this to raise money to build houses.

Three of the first Quichua church leaders in Colta, Manuel Bueno, Nicholas Lamar and Manuel Bahua Cajas, all testified to having profound spiritual experiences at an evangelistic street meeting in Guayaquil. Other Quichuas had similar experiences at evangelistic meetings in that city.

Previously, the only Spanish whites the Chimborazo

85

Quichuas had known were Roman Catholics. They were impressed to see Spanish people in evangelical churches on the coast and holding their evangelical weddings, baptisms and other services with practically no opposition.

## Indian rights

In the mid-1960s, Quichuas were beginning to get their own land. They were feeling less control from the Roman Catholic hierarchy. And they were getting a better education and exposure to new ideas. So it was only natural that Quichuas felt a greater sense of their own rights.

The secular Quichuas expressed their rights by fighting for land and getting increasingly involved in politics. The Quichua evangelicals were feeling more sure of themselves now that they had their own Association. The 300 or so baptized church members developed expressions of "Quichua-ness."

Before, the few Quichua believers felt intimidated by the political and religious leaders. Now they were beginning to stand up for their beliefs.

In the early 1960s, the Quichua believers built several more church buildings similar to the first one in El Troje. New converts maintained a steady and aggressive witness. Manuel Bueno of Colta for several years maintained a grueling preaching schedule. Every Sunday he preached at three different churches—El Troje, Pulucate and Caliata—walking a total of six hours to make all those stops.

Children accepted the Lord at the boarding school, and the missionaries made evangelistic contacts with the parents. People who never would have entered a church made decisions of faith while listening to the Quichuas' evangelical radio station.

## Shattering the stereotypes

Land and Catholic reform. Increased mobility. Indian rights. Lay and missionary witness. Many factors combined to create greater Quichua openness to the gospel. But people were also becoming Christians in ways that defied explanation and shattered all stereotypes.

One Sunday a rugged-looking fellow wearing chaps entered the Colta church midway through the preaching service. The visitor waited a few moments before raising his hand to speak. But no one acknowledged him. Finally, the man announced for all to hear, "I have come to become an evangelical."

All heads turned in his direction.

"I've heard about this on the radio, and I want to become a Christian. Now, please. I have to walk at least two hours to get back home, and I want to get there before dark. Can I become a Christian right now?"

The missionaries in attendance watched to see how the Quichua preacher would handle such a petition. And as if it were the most natural request in the world, the speaker immediately stopped his message.

"Of course you can," he said, pointing to a deacon in the front row. "Pray with him."

Then, eyeing the rest of the congregation, the preacher added, "And if anyone else would like to pray the same prayer of salvation, please go down now and join the deacon."

Amazed by the scene unfolding before them, the missionaries counted at least five or six more who went forward. Later, while the missionaries discussed that day's worship service, some wondered aloud, "Can a person really make a Christian commitment with so little Bible knowledge?"

Missionaries and Quichua believers alike questioned if they would ever see the man in church again. But their doubts flew out the church door several weeks later, when the same man returned. And this time he brought a dozen people with him.

"They want to accept the Lord too," he said. "I've explained to them what happened to me, and I'm so happy that I'm a child of God and that I'm on my way to heaven, I want these people to have salvation explained to them too."

## Is today the day?

God moved in ways which seemed to go against everything the missionaries knew. Henry Klassen witnessed to a man who said he wanted to become a Christian; however, the man said he still had two more feast obligations to fulfill.

"Make your decision now," Henry urged. "The Bible says today is the day of salvation."

"I'm sorry," said Jorge [not his real name]. "But I can't do it yet."

Several years later, Henry was driving down the road when he again saw Jorge, dressed in a devil's outfit made from sheepskin and horsehair. He was surrounded by a crowd of Quichua fiesta-goers. Jorge was obviously drunk, but he recognized the missionary and motioned him over.

Jorge leaned his bleary eyes toward Henry's car window and said, "When my obligations are over, I'm going to become a Christian."

Another year passed, and Jorge's wife and daughter paid Henry a visit. It was Saturday night and fiesta time once again.

The women said, "Jorge sent us to tell you that tomorrow he's going to become a Christian at the church."

"Where is he now?" asked Henry.

"He's down getting drunk."

Sure enough, the next day Jorge appeared in the Colta church and made his profession of faith. Henry was definitely skeptical about the way it was done, but he could not dispute the end result. Jorge stood firm as a new Christian.

Again Klassen was surprised when God seemed to use even dreams to win Quichuas to himself. Until now, the missionary saw dreams more as the result of eating disagreeable food, not divine communication.

Then he met Pedro, a local Quichua who consistently prohibited his wife and children from going to church. One night Pedro beat his wife after learning she had sneaked out to church. Then he stumbled into bed drunk.

That night Pedro dreamed that flames were consuming his body. He could see people at the evangelical church, and he called for them to save him. However, the people said it was impossible for them to save him. Pedro would have to escape the fire by coming to them.

Pedro awoke in a holy terror that frightened away his hangover. For him, the interpretation was obvious: God was giving him one last chance to escape hellfire.

The following Sunday Pedro took his whole family to the little church. Each one went forward to publicly receive Christ as Savior. Pedro had his spiritual ups and downs after accepting the Lord, but everyone pointed to that Sunday when Pedro's life turned around.

The missionaries had labored for decades with few visible results. Now it seemed like God was saying, "Thank-you everybody. Now move over and let me go to work."

# 13

# FISHERMEN AND INCAS

In one year's time, from 1969 to 1970, the number of Quichua evangelicals doubled in Chimborazo Province. Now there were at least 1,600 baptized church members. The missionaries knew that if the churches kept growing, as they hoped they would, the Quichuas would have to perform the tasks of ordained pastors.

The handful of missionaries was not going to be around Chimborazo forever, and even if they were, they could not possibly visit the growing number of churches and preaching points.

Yet each time the matter came up, the Quichua believers insisted they were not educated or capable enough.

"But of course you're educated enough," Henry Klassen would say. "Look, I'm just an ordinary farmer like most of you."

"Yes, but even if we became pastors, no one would respect us," they said.

"You're comparing yourselves to the priests with all their formal education," Henry would argue. "It's not necessary to have all those degrees to pastor a church. Of course, you must know your Bible and be a mature Christian leader. But many of you already meet those qualifications."

There were some very practical reasons for having Quichua pastors. Who else would conduct the baptisms, weddings, funerals and worship services for the growing number of believers?

Maybe Quichua pastors would make mistakes, but so did all new church leaders. Having Quichua pastors leading Quichua churches would make it worth risking some errors, GMU missionaries felt. The mission had adopted the policy that Quichuas must build their own church buildings without mission financial support, and Quichua believers already worked as announcers at the radio station. One taught at the boarding school. They had proven themselves as effective preachers and evangelists. So it seemed only natural that mature Quichua leaders assume the reins as ordained pastors as well.

The new Quichua believers had consistently proven how fast they could learn. A missionary from World Radio HCJB in Quito had challenged one of the boarding school students, young José Juan Naula, to write a fifteen-minute radio program.

"Include the music, Scripture, preaching and poetry, and bring it to me tomorrow," said the missionary.

José Juan found Klassen later that day. "I can't do it," he said glumly.

"Sure you can, José Juan."

"But I don't even know what poetry is."

"Yes, you do. Remember how we were studying the Psalms? That's poetry."

That part made sense to José Juan. But he left shaking his head. Him—prepare a radio program?

Into the late hours of the night, José Juan helped his father thrash barley, but the whole time his mind was working. The next morning he went to the HCJB missionary with a program. Not only that, he showed her an original song with three stanzas and a chorus based on Genesis 1:1. The first stanza went:

"We see Father God's handiwork
His work is seen in this world
He made all things beautiful
The sun and the moon he has made."

José Juan sang his song, and everyone immediately fell

in love with it. His "Creation Song" swept the tiny Quichua congregations, who, for the first time, sang a hymn written by one of their own.

Seeing what José Juan had done, other Quichua believers, including José Juan's brother Manuel, started writing songs. The two brothers and Manuel Naula Sagñay, an up-and-coming Christian leader from Pulucate who taught at the boarding school in Colta, formed a trio that became an instant sensation over the Quichua radio station.

It was a liberating moment for the young Quichua church. No longer did they have to depend on translated Spanish or English hymns. They had their own music. They could put Christian words to the native melodies and attract a hearing among the non-Christian Quichuas.

## Matter of necessity

Almost by necessity, the Quichua church leaders took their first steps toward leadership. During a time when Henry Klassen was on furlough and the only other male missionaries in Colta spoke only Spanish, Mary Warkentine got into a discussion with several Quichua leaders in Colta about the church leadership needs.

The Quichuas voiced their opinion that only missionaries should perform pastoral functions.

"Look, brothers," said the normally soft-spoken missionary with force that surprised the Quichua men. "What kind of men did Jesus leave behind to do his work?"

She read from Acts 4:13: "Now when they saw the boldness of Peter and John, and perceived that they were uneducated, common men, they wondered; and they recognized that they had been with Jesus."

Her listeners seemed to grasp the significance of the passage. And from then on, they showed new willingness to get involved in church leadership.

A similar instance occurred in Caliata, where two Quichua leaders there requested the help of missionaries stationed in Colta. Carl McMindes of GMU discussed the matter with them, and he went down the list of Colta-based

GMU missionaries, one by one. To transfer any of them would mean the end or reduction of an existing ministry in Colta, McMindes pointed out.

Seeing that, the Caliata leaders agreed, "I guess we'll have to do the work ourselves."

Afterward, McMindes called this an "exciting experience" repeated on several occasions. "I will admit that as our missionary force [among the Quichuas] got smaller, the national church leadership got larger and stronger and began to assume more and more of the responsibility."

**God uses the ordinary**

Quichuas' resistance to church leadership particularly frustrated Klassen, who felt he was living proof that God can use the ordinary man in Christian ministry.

Just when it had seemed like he and Pat were on their way to the mission field, the old objections about Henry's supposed lack of qualifications had risen again.

The mission cook doubted whether Henry's sensitive stomach could handle spicy, unfamiliar foreign foods and predicted he would never last in another country. True, a childhood illness had restricted his diet, but Henry believed God could take care of him in as small a matter as food.

Then came the question of education. "I don't think he can learn another language," said a board member.

"I believe he can," contradicted another. He knew Henry had grown up speaking low German and had already learned English as a second language.

"But he's only got a seventh-grade education. Besides, he'll need to learn not only Spanish, but Quichua."

"I'm sure he can do it," affirmed the other.

The mission board finally accepted Henry, but on the grounds that before leaving the country he must pass his high school equivalency tests. It was hard—chemistry and other subjects kept Henry up past midnight many times. But he finished in a year.

Henry and Pat then completed the deputation process, in which they obtained pledges of financial support for their work. During this preparation time, they also became proud parents of a son, Darrel.

As the family went through the final farewells before leaving for Ecuador, one last objection came up.

"I don't want to hear that one of my sons can't provide for his wife and family," said Henry's father, skeptical of his son's venture, and not a little disappointed that Henry had not become the farmer he had raised him to be.

"Don't worry, Dad. Churches and friends will be supporting me."

"You'll get down to Ecuador and they'll forget. Out of sight, out of mind."

"No, they won't." Henry explained he merely intended to obey the call of God to go to the Quichuas. He had no illusions of greatness or secret ambitions. He only wanted to serve the Lord as best he knew how.

"I really believe God can use the ordinary layman," Henry told Pat. "God wouldn't have led us to Ecuador for no reason."

### Descendants of the Incas

Leading his weekly Bible study in El Troje, Klassen mentioned to attenders that in the near future, few if any male missionaries would be around. Some were going on furlough. Others had moved elsewhere.

He himself might have to fill in at his mission's Quito office. Who, then, would perform the Quichuas' weddings, burials and increasing baptisms if not the Quichuas themselves?

The El Troje believers had led the way in the Quichua church movement. Many of his listeners had a mature faith, tested by persecution. Klassen knew that El Troje could supply an adequate pastoral candidate—or candidates.

Klassen caught Matías Mullo's eye. Matías, for instance, seemed a natural candidate for pastor. He and Matías had become close friends over the years. Matías's gentle nature and sense of humor combined with a deep faith and pastoral gifts. If Matías did not qualify for spiritual leadership, then who did? Suddenly inspired, Klassen said vigorously, "Look at you. You are Quichua Indians—descendants of the proud Incas."

The Bible class seemed to pay renewed attention.

"In some ways you are like the people of Israel. The Israelites fell under the authority of Egypt, but they remained God's chosen people and God used them.

"You, the Incas, fell under the domination of the Spaniards. You, too, are still a special people. And God wants to use you."

The missionary paused, letting that sink in. "I believe God wants some of you to become ordained pastors."

"But most of us haven't even passed the third grade," someone mumbled.

"You can do it," Henry persisted. "Very soon there may not be any foreign missionaries to baptize your new believers or to perform the other duties of a pastor."

"Well, if you won't do it, we'll go ask the priests," blurted one listener.

The comment shocked everyone. But without skipping a beat, Klassen said, "If your faith goes no farther than that, well, that's another matter entirely." Looking directly at Matías, he added, "And I know you do have a strong faith."

This time no one said anything.

"Don't you see that Jesus used humble men who worked with their hands to build his church?" Klassen continued. "Jesus chose fishermen, men who worked with their hands. Some probably couldn't read or write. Don't you think Jesus can use you, too?"

By now, the missionary had about exhausted his arguments. He scanned the faces of his listeners. Suddenly, Matías's eyes shone like the sun rising over Lake Colta, and he rose from his seat.

"If fishermen could carry on the Lord's work," he said, appealing to the men seated around him, "then so can we."

**Taking the initiative**

With the support of Matías and other key leaders, the

missionaries began preparing a training course for pastors. Three men studied in the first group: the two brothers, José Juan and Manuel Naula, and Manuel Bueno. Matías joined a second group of candidates.

Even as he prepared for ordination, José Juan helped the missionaries with the Bible teaching. One Saturday he went ahead into the village of Miraflor to prepare some forty candidates for their baptism the following day by the missionaries.

When two carloads of missionaries and Quichua believers drove to Miraflor on Sunday, an angry mob turned them back.

"We're not going to let you bring heresy into this area," they said. Most were drunk, and they threatened to beat the visitors if they did not leave. That night back in Colta, everyone worried about José Juan. Had the mob gone into Miraflor and beaten him?

But the next day, excited messengers came with big news: "José Juan went ahead with the baptism anyway!"

The young preacher had been informed of the disturbance taking place. So, while trouble surged down the mountain from Miraflor, he went ahead with the baptism—ordination or no ordination.

Not only the missionaries took note of his surprising initiative. So did the Miraflor non-Christians. One later told Klassen, "We found that even if we stopped the missionaries, we couldn't stop what you were teaching."

On May 23, 1971, José Juan became "official," along with his brother, Manuel, and Manuel Bueno during an ordination service at the Colta church. About 400 Quichua believers and some misty-eyed missionaries looked on. They sensed the historic nature of the day. The ordination joined the string of many recent firsts: the first believers, the first baptism, the first church building and now the first Quichua pastors.

It would take these and many more Quichua pastors and leaders to keep pace with exploding growth in the churches.

# CHAIN REACTION

It was such a small thing—trading a Bible for a whip. Henry Klassen never dreamed what was going to happen.

Selling Bibles as usual in the Sunday market in nearby Cajabamba, the missionary noticed a middle-aged Quichua man eyeing his stock. The man could not seem to make up his mind whether he wanted to buy a Bible. So Henry went ahead and encouraged him to do so.

As the two men talked, Henry learned that his potential customer was a leatherworker skilled in making whips. Henry thought about offering the man a Bible for nothing, but he also knew that people rarely valued things they got for free.

"Why don't we make a deal?" Klassen said. "One of these Bibles for one of your whips?"

The idea appealed to the Quichua man, who then introduced himself as Pablo Añilema from San Bernardo. Henry knew the area, south of Colta. There was no evangelical church all through the valley leading to San Bernardo. The village lay near Columbe, that old center of evangelical opposition and liquor hangouts, which seemed to block entry of the gospel to the region.

Henry did not really expect to see or hear from the leatherworker again. But one day Pablo came looking for him.

"I've been reading this Bible and sharing what it says with all my friends and family," Pablo began.

"Do you understand what you're reading?" Henry asked.

"Most of it. But I've heard that you have movies about this Jesus mentioned in the Bible. Would you come to San Bernardo and show us some of those films?"

"Why, I guess that could be arranged," Henry said, his heart pounding. What an opening this would be! Many times the films had gotten the missionaries into places that would have never permitted an ordinary preacher.

On faith, Henry had purchased an expensive set of films on the life of Christ, and he had not regretted it. For believers who could not read, the films functioned as well as a Bible study. And for nonbelievers, the films communicated with the same effect as a skilled evangelist.

Klassen invited Manuel Naula, the recently-ordained Quichua pastor, and his wife, Lorenza, to accompany him. Once in San Bernardo, the Naulas began singing hymns and choruses, attracting a large crowd to the meeting place beside the local school. Meanwhile, Klassen sold Christian books and literature.

As the afternoon wore on, the crowd kept growing. And Henry quickly exhausted his supply of literature. It was easy to see Pablo Añilema had done lots of promotion before the missionaries arrived.

Things rolled along smoothly until the time for the films. Henry planned to show two of the movies about Christ, and he was getting things ready when Manuel Naula brought some disturbing news.

"The people are saying that drunks have cut a trench in the road so we can't get out," Manuel said. "People say the hole is at least a meter deep. Do you think we should make a run for it across the mountains while we still have the chance?"

Henry had observed some raucous drinkers on the way into San Bernardo, but until now he had not thought much about them.

"Maybe *you* can outrun them, but I can't," Henry said. "Besides, I've already got the film equipment set up, and I don't want to leave it behind. There must be 300 people waiting for our meeting. Why don't you go ahead and preach?"

Manuel met the missionary's gaze, then he turned around and headed back to the crowd. That night he preached like Henry had never heard him before. It was a stirring call to Christian commitment.

"Even though the world may be against us, Christ is with us," Manuel preached, obviously with the drunken mob in the back of his mind.

When Manuel delivered the invitation to accept Christ, a number of hands went up. However, the darkness made it difficult to count how many. The Quichua pastor asked everyone who had raised their hands to join him in a common prayer for salvation. After that Henry showed the two movies. It was at least midnight when they finished.

"Why don't you stay overnight?" asked Pablo Añilema and some of the others. "It will be easier to get out in the daylight."

Figuring the drunks might come after them before morning, Henry declined. So some of the men volunteered to go on ahead and inspect the extent of the road's damage. They returned in about an hour with the good news that they had filled in the trench. Henry and the Naulas could leave.

"And the mob?" Henry asked.

"There are only about seventy of them and 300 of us," they said. "We'll send 150 people ahead of your car and put another 150 or so behind you.

"We'll also put a few men above the road, and they'll make sure that no one tries to shove rocks down the mountain onto the car."

As Henry got into his jeep to leave, a man poked his face by the window. "Can you come back and show the films again?"

"That depends on whether we get out or not," Henry said.

"We do want you to come back," the same man continued. "I'm not an evangelical, but I'm not as fanatical as that mob."

Slowly, cautiously, the jeep and its human convoy

moved into the darkness and down the rutted trail leading away from San Bernardo. To everyone's relief, they reached the main road without encountering the mob. The Quichua "bodyguards" bade farewell, since it was home free from then on.

"How many do you suppose raised their hands?" Henry asked Manuel after the initial tension had worn off.

"I don't want to exaggerate, but I would say as many as fifty," Manuel said.

Henry nodded his head. That was about as many as he had thought. Even if there were only thirty or forty, that was thirty or forty more believers than before the preaching and film showing.

## Faith spreads amid persecution

Klassen and Naula did not know it, but their evangelistic foray into San Bernardo particularly stirred the heart of the whipseller's brother, Agustín Añilema.

A practicing Catholic, Agustín regularly prayed before going to bed. And one night during prayers, he felt a heavy depression.

"I will have to meet God some day," he thought. "I get along well with with my Spanish bosses and with my fellow Quichuas. But when I die, my soul will be worth nothing before God. God will ask me what I have been doing, and I won't be able to answer him."

Agustín wept bitterly at the thought. What was especially bad, he did not know who could help him.

Agustín started listening to the Quichua Christian radio station. He bought a Bible and tried unsuccessfully to understand the book of Genesis. He even stopped drinking, and people accused him of being an evangelical.

Then came the film showing. Full of questions after seeing the movies, Agustín went to Klassen on the pretext of getting the missionary to fix his radio. Klassen knew little about radios, so he sent Añilema to Quichua church leader Manuel Bueno, who did.

The two men discussed the gospel. Soon after Agustín

100

went to one of the Bible institute classes in Colta and prayed to receive Christ.

Agustín began witnessing wherever he went—on the road, in the buses and among his friends and relatives. His brother, Pablo, also made a profession of faith. And before long, a group of evangelicals was meeting regularly for worship in San Bernardo. Not only that, they preached to neighbors up and down the long valley from their village.

Before long, the inevitable opposition arose. The San Bernardo believers were threatened and harrassed. Pablo and Agustín, respected leaders in their community, filed grievances against their persecutors in nearby Columbe.

When a man named Ignacio Lema, who lived in a village farther up the valley, professed faith in Christ, some of the San Bernardo believers went to visit and encourage him. However, these San Bernardo believers were taken prisoner at the local hacienda. The persecutors forced them to bathe and then beat their wet skin with cactus nettles.

The Añilemas and other San Bernardo believers heard about the incident, and they went for the police in Riobamba. However, the police could do little against a drunken fiesta mob of 700. Agustín and some of the believers were roughed up, but they felt thankful to get out alive.

Agustín and the others then asked Henry Klassen to take them to the authorities in Riobamba. This time when police went to the hacienda, they were able to capture the ringleaders. More persecution followed, but the churches continued to grow. Soon the missionaries would find out just how much.

## Unforgettable baptism

Roughly fourteen months after that first film showing, the San Bernardo believers asked the missionaries to conduct a baptismal service for them.

Manuel Naula and another Quichua leader went to San Bernardo two days early to hear the testimonies of the baptismal candidates and to prepare them for the service on Sunday.

When some of the the missionaries went to the village for the baptism, Manuel hurried over to Klassen with some exciting news.

"Remember how we thought that fifty people raised their hands?" he said. "There are 155 people ready to be baptized and most of them date their decision back to that night we showed the film."

The local believers had dammed off the mountain stream, creating five different pools. The baptismal candidates divided into five lines, one for each pool. Three missionaries and two Quichua pastors performed the baptisms in the rushing icy water, while a huge crowd perched on the steep banks. After the baptism, everyone walked back up the hill to the church for the communion service.

Missionary Mary Warkentine, observing the scene, wrote later, "Too many to crowd into the church, they stood outside. Row upon row. Oblivious to the frequent, but heavy, showers of rain. There was a deep undercurrent of joy in that congregation that was unmistakeable and infectious."

The missionaries returned to Colta "with a thrilling assurance that we had been in the presence of God," said Warkentine. "What more can we ask for to make life rich and meaningful?"

**Missionary zeal**

In a matter of months after the 1971 baptism, almost the entire community of San Bernardo became evangelicals. In fact, some of the believers told Klassen they had no one left to witness to.

"Why don't you go to the other communities?" he suggested.

"We don't know if it would be wise to go uninvited into strange communities," they said.

"But what if we missionaries had used the same excuse?" Klassen said. "We didn't know anyone when we came to Ecuador, and no one was interested in listening to us." The San Bernardo leaders said they understood what Henry meant.

Not long after this discussion, a week-long Bible institute took place in Colta. By now, the missionaries were holding four institutes per year as a way to disciple and train the many new Christians. It surprised everyone when the San Bernardo group did not show up. Because of the persecution, attenders feared for the believers' safety.

Then, toward the end of the week, some San Bernardo church leaders straggled in with beaming smiles.

"Instead of coming straight to the institute," they said, "we decided to take a week and visit some of the Quichuas in Bolívar Province," they said.

The San Bernardo church had chosen twelve members to participate in their first-ever missionary journey. To them, twelve seemed the biblical number.

During their trip, the San Bernardo missionaries found listeners very receptive; many had never heard the gospel before. When some of the Bolívar Quichuas gave the visitors additional food for their journey, the group extended their trip. That was why they had arrived late for the institute.

San Bernardo-area believers continued to aggressively preach the gospel, which propelled from village to village back through the valley. Always, the first believers in a community suffered persecution. Rarely, however, did the opposition keep them from meeting and witnessing.

In one village in the valley, a local religious authority and the landowner called a meeting for local Quichuas to plot how to get rid of the evangelicals. The conspirators' meeting was scheduled for a building on the hacienda. However, two days before the meeting, heavy rains caused a landslide that crashed into the hacienda and sent its buildings into the river below.

To the opposition, this natural disaster seemed like a direct revelation from God. They wanted no more part in opposing the evangelicals if this was how God protected them. From then on, evangelicals encountered no more opposition in this part of the valley.

103

## "Hotel" Rodeopamba

Two years from the time he had traded that Bible to Pablo Añilema for a whip, Henry Klassen received a preaching invitation from believers in Rodeopamba. Klassen had never been there before. It was the final village before the rising San Bernardo valley ended at the treeless, grassy plateau more than 13,000 feet above sea level.

Henry drove his jeep until the dirt road ended. Then he traveled the rest of the way by horseback. Thrilled the missionary had traveled so far to visit them, the Quichua believers received Klassen as if he were royalty.

When the meetings continued through 11:00 p.m., Klassen found his head nodding, and he asked to be excused from the meeting. His Quichua hosts quipped that Klassen's "hotel room" was ready, and they took him to a pile of fresh hay in a mud hut. Klassen, who often said that the prerequisite for any missionary is "being able to sleep anywhere, any place, any time," found his accomodations as comfortable as the Hilton, and he fell asleep.

It was a short night, however, because the men shook him from a deep sleep at 4:00 a.m. "It's time for another service," they told him.

"At this hour?" asked the groggy missionary.

"Yes, we want you to show those slides you brought along before it gets daylight."

And so the meetings continued until breakfast. Afterward, Henry and a Quichua pastor baptized thirty believers in the frigid mountain stream. Then everyone headed back up the hill for communion and dedication of their new church.

Amazed by the vitality of this new church, Klassen asked the leaders how it started. "Everything began with a potato merchant," they said.

The vendor had come to their village, testifying about Christ while selling his wares. His preaching had angered the community leaders, who considered doing away with him. However, they kept listening to the fearless mer-

104

chant's words all through the night. By morning the village leaders found themselves agreeing that maybe there really was a better way of life than feasting and fighting. They chose Christ as the answer.

## Mission field to mission force

After so many years of trying to get even one church started, the missionaries now found themselves hopping to keep pace with their Quichua Christian brothers and sisters. Increasingly, the missionaries found themselves in a support role, with the Quichuas on the front lines. The "witnessed to" had become the witnesses.

When Gospel Missionary Union entered Ecuador at the turn of the century, Will Reed said, "Ecuador will never be evangelized by outsiders." That prophecy appeared to hold true for the Quichuas. The missionaries had initiated many things, but Quichua lay witnesses were making the church grow.

One night Henry Klassen and José Juan Naula stood above the Colta mission station. It was Carnival, and they could see drunken feasting in full swing.

"If it weren't for the Gospel, I'd be right down there with them," José Juan said. "Now I have purpose for living. Not only in this life, but for the hereafter." He wiped away a tear.

"We have found something worthwhile," he continued. "We have found something that our forefathers searched for, but they did not find. I praise God that we found it in our day. Now it's up to us to proclaim it to others."

# 15

# THE NEW INCAS

In 1975 former Gospel Missionary Union director G. Christian Weiss decided to make a return visit to Chimborazo Province. Little more than twenty years had passed since he and other mission leaders had seriously considered terminating the Quichua work.

All that Weiss could remember about Chimborazo were drunken brawls and zero membership rolls. Now he was hearing good reports from the missionaries there. But how much had things really changed?

Arriving in Chimborazo, Weiss visited villages where missionaries had worked decades without forming even a small nucleus of Quichua believers. Now churches were filled to overflowing.

The Quichua evangelical church had skyrocketed to an estimated 7,000 baptized members, missionaries told Weiss. This compared to only 250 baptized believers less than ten years before.

The overall worshiping community was estimated at 20,000. In other words, believers and sympathizers totaled roughly ten percent of the entire Quichua population of Chimborazo.

In many Chimborazo villages, from eighty to ninety percent of the population were evangelicals. The old adobe huts in many of these villages had disappeared as thrifty industrious new believers used money previously spent on

106

feasting to build concrete-block houses.

Seeing the transformation of Chimborazo and the Quichua people, Weiss blinked back tears. He felt mixed emotions of wonder and relief.

"The question came to me with tremendous force: What if we had given up?" he wrote after his trip.

"I am more convinced than I have ever been that no people in the world are beyond the reach of God's great love nor beyond the power of His glorious gospel."

## A culture transformed

"Change" is a dirty word for many anthropologists and sociologists. They often accuse Western missionaries of destroying or "changing" indigenous cultures. (Meanwhile, they ignore that missionaries, through reducing a tribal group's language to writing and translating Scripture, do more to preserve a culture than any anthropologist might hope to accomplish.)

Because of the tensions, missionaries often avoid the word "change," when they describe what God's saving power does in a person or people group. For them, "transformation" is a safer word.

Call it change, transform, alter or metamorphose. But anyone visiting Chimborazo Province in the mid-1970s realized something was going on there. The lives of hundreds, and then thousands, of Quichuas were . . . well, *changed* after their conversion to Christianity. And so, whole villages and customs were *transformed*.

You did not have to be a sociology major to perceive the difference between what the Quichua Christians were before and what they had become.

An Ecuadorian military officer commented to Henry Klassen, "We used to treat the Indians like animals. But now you evangelicals have made something out of them. We have to start treating them like people."

On another occasion, Klassen's jeep got stuck on one of the muddy, back roads. He asked a local Quichua man to help, and the two men started visiting. "Yeah, we don't

107

have enough evangelicals here yet," the man said, implying evangelicals were the only ones who fixed their roads.

The village of Columbe, that popular drinking hole for thousands of Quichuas and hub of activity for legal and church matters, became practically a ghost town. One of the big universities blamed Columbe's demise on the evangelicals, saying they were anti-progressive.

But what had happened was the surrounding Quichua believers no longer had any reason to spend their money in Columbe. They neither bought liquor nor celebrated the feasts. They had their own churches, cemeteries, stores and schools. For them, it was as if Columbe no longer existed.

One of the provincial authorities told Klassen that the chief law enforcement agent in Columbe might be relocated to another area: there was not enough to keep him busy. Klassen appreciated the significance of the man's statement, but told him even evangelicals sometimes have problems and need legal attention.

Once Quichuas were transformed spiritually, they became open to new vistas of every kind.

"One of the hardest barriers to cross is the spiritual one," said Phil Westra, a Luke Society missionary who organized agricultural projects for the Quichuas in the early 1980s. "Getting someone to accept a latrine, health or agricultural project is easy compared to a spiritual change.

"But once this spiritual change is made, other changes may be less threatening. The advance of the gospel has prepared the way for the kind of work [social and development projects] you see now."

**The question is why**

What explained the Quichuas' sudden transformation? Why, after so many years of unresponsiveness, were Quichuas suddenly turning to the gospel? The answer remained a mystery even for many of the Quichua believers.

During his 1976 furlough, Henry Klassen did graduate studies in the area of world missions. For a class project, he chose to analyze the spectacular growth of the Quichua churches.

As he thought back over his twenty-three years in Ecuador, Klassen could not single out one reason for the growth. Many factors had contributed, but one of the biggest was the policy of giving Quichua believers their own churches and encouraging them to develop their own leaders and worship style.

Klassen had never ordered the Quichua leaders to do anything. He tried to give them ownership in decisions. In fact, the Quichua believers had assumed control and responsibility before many observers thought they were ready. With God's help, the leaders had proven themselves capable.

The mission had decided not to send potential pastors to seminary far away. There had not been time for that. Instead, they tried to provide church leaders with "on-the-job" training. The churches were growing so fast, pastors were needed right then.

Also, Klassen appreciated the team concept, which had guided the work of the missionaries over the years. It had taken every one of them to do the job.

The growth had taken place without a lot of dollars and bricks. A missionary from another agency told Klassen, "I'm jealous. We've spent thousands of dollars, and we still don't have anything to show for our work."

As far as methods, the missionaries had used radio, the medical work, Christian films, and even a canvas tent for church conferences. They also obtained vehicles to travel to outlying villages and other tools of modern technology.

Of course, translated Scriptures played a big part. Mrs. Woodward's original New Testament translation was revised, and the new version was dedicated in a 1973 ceremony drawing more than 4,500 people.

The mission's Bible institutes and theological education by extension classes had grounded the new believers in Scripture and made them effective witnesses.

And (as described earlier in this book), factors such as land reform and Vatican II played a part. Most important, perhaps, was the matter of God's sovereignty. It was God's time for the Quichuas. It was like Klassen's missiology professor Ralph Winter had said, "The moment you start *planning* a people movement, it peters out."

## Quichuas explain the change

I asked many of the Quichua leaders to explain Chimborazo's spiritual revival of the 1960s and 1970s. Manuel Bueno, one of the original believers in Colta, said his faith had really taken root in the Columbe jail, where he was held briefly with the El Troje believers. In the jail he realized he could not return to what he was. "I knew the Lord had taken control of my life."

Among the possible reasons for Quichua church growth, he listed: 1) the persecution, which caused political authorities to see the Gospel really was not a threat to anyone; 2) the witness of the changed lives of the believers; 3) a soccer team, composed of believers from San Antonio and Majipamba, who distributed tracts and witnessed wherever they played; 4) the conferences and film showings; 5) the active lay witness of new believers and the San Antonio merchants.

Manuel Naula Yupangui, with Bueno one of the first three ordained Quichua pastors who later became a lawyer in Quito, traced the growth to "pastoral leadership and the fact that everything was dedicated to evangelism." Also, the people who most opposed the evangelicals either converted or died, he said.

Manuel Naula Sagñay, former teacher at the Colta boarding school who became the first Quichua medical doctor, mentioned as reasons for the spiritual revival: 1) the visible change in the conduct of new believers, who caused others to seek the same kind of change; 2) the enthusiasm of new believers to testify to their relatives, friends and neighbors; 3) the conversions of influential leaders in the different Quichua communities; and 4) the fact that Quichuas themselves preached and performed their music in the churches and over the radio.

The widening generation gap between young and old Quichua believers constituted probably the biggest challenge facing the church, said Naula. The clash between generations is also a cultural clash, the doctor said. "It's a conflict in which Quichua young people don't know or don't realize what culture they really belong to, the Quichua or the Spanish.

"The churches must give these young people the opportunity to participate as leaders. This is denied in some churches, and it explains the frequent difficulties between young people and adults."

**Scholarly analyses**

William Reyburn of the United Bible Societies, who lived in the Colta area from 1952-1955 and after 1979 made periodic visits to work with the Old Testament translation committee, said, "The story as I have seen and heard it over a period of years is not at all simple, but just the same it retains that dimension of mystery that God seems to delight us mortals with."

In Reyburn's view, the major factor in the spiritual breakthrough was land reform. "The breaking up of some large land holdings in the Colta-Cajabamba area by the military regime gave the Indians of those areas a chance to obtain freedom in the form of land ownership," he said.

"The land was made available for sale. This meant money was needed. But money was spent on the acquisition of status through the church-related fiesta system.

"The evangelical system was highly individualized: an individual salvation, an individual education for reading one's own book and, most importantly, the evangelical church had no money-consuming fiestas.

"In short, here was the Good News of freedom being preached, an education in a book and an escape from the fiesta system allowing one to save his money. The evangelical church fit the rise of the wave of materialism that was to engulf the people and later the very church. Every leader I know points to materialism and money as the major points of tension in the church today.

"Money saved was for purchasing land made available by the military government. So, for the Quichua, everything pivoted on the rights of land and from this, poured forth a whole rainbow of related factors."

Reyburn also signaled the importance of Scripture for Quichua evangelicals. "The importance of a book-related Christianity, (which distinguished it clearly from the Roman Catholic church), has been at the front since the beginning and it will continue to be," he said.

## Social developments

Noted evangelical writer and linguist Eugene Nida of the American Bible Society pointed to social and political developments, which influenced church growth in Chimborazo.

"Back in 1947 when my wife and I were first in the area, Indians were almost entirely controlled by the hacienda system," he said. "There was little or no political involvement of the Indian constituency, and by and large the Indians had retreated to a socially defensive position in order to maintain some semblance of their cultural heritage.

"There have been radical changes in Indian society, particularly in view of some of the economic growth in which Indians have developed industry, especially weaving.... Moreover, Indian men have been traveling from region to region in Ecuador, and many have traveled abroad. This has given them a realization of what life can and should be."

He also said that in any mass movement, "So much depends upon individual leadership by charismatic persons.... People with great leadership potential who are touched by the power of the Holy Spirit in their lives can do unusual and unexpected things. Therefore it seems to me it is impossible in certain circumstances to predict what is going to happen, given certain social and political developments. God still works through individuals."

## Culture or Christian?

Different observers also cautioned against sensationalizing the Quichuas' story. Dick Farstad, skilled linguist and formerly of World Radio HCJB's Quichua language service, observed in the early 1980s that "a lot of people have come into the movement, but we don't know how many of those people are really Christian. And if they're all Christians, many are very shallow."

He complimented Gospel Missionary Union's good job of teaching and discipling the believers, while noting there were thousands who still had not attended the Bible institutes or classes.

Some Quichuas had confused going forward in an altar call as not only giving them salvation in Christ, but also giving them membership in the church association, a job and other benefits.

Farstad said the question needed to be asked, "Is it just a subculture or is it really something spiritual—a work of the Holy Spirit? I guess as I see it, it's a little of both. One of the secrets in Chimborazo is that the culture has been respected—in the dress, the lifestyle, the church building doesn't have to be square or have seats.... I'm sure a lot of the young people are just swept into the church because it's the thing to do."

## The New Incas

Seen within its larger context, the Chimborazo Quichua story became part of a larger movement of God in the South American Andes.

Church growth also took place among the Quichuas of Ecuador's northern Imbabura province, where the dialect differs slightly from the Quichua of Chimborazo. From 1916 to 1969, there were never more than twenty-eight baptized Quichua believers, said David Volstad of the Christian and Missionary Alliance denomination working among them. By 1979, there were at least 900 believers, and the figure kept growing.

Literally thousands of Peruvian and Bolivian Quechuas joined the evangelical ranks in the 1960s and 1970s. As in Ecuador, church growth in these two countries came after the adoption of land reform legislation and with the diffusion of Scripture in their native tongues.

Though the Spaniards crushed the once-proud Incas, they did not destroy the identity of the Andean people, who still retain an underlying cultural affinity and collective memory of sorts. (The Quichua and Quechua language families in the Andes Mountains may embrace up to 14 million people, said Dick Farstad. He knew of at least nineteen different Quechua dialects in Peru and eight Ecuadorian Quichua dialects.)

Curiously, the Inca prophets used to talk about a coming new age, when the Incas would rise again with new life and freedom from oppression. At least for Chimborazo Quichuas and other Andean Christians, new life has already come.

Several well-placed Ecuadorian officials once offered a Colta Quichua a lucrative job if he would leave evangelicalism. "Why don't you forget about the evangelicals?" they asked. "They just talk a mystical religion full of false promises. We can give you something good right now."

The Quichua believer at first did not know how to respond. Then he remembered to pray and the answer came.

"Look. You are making fun of what I believe. You may not believe in the Bible. But I want you to know one thing. Jesus has changed my life so completely, I never want to go back to what I was before. Why should I go against my faith?"

The men never bothered him again. He was a "new Inca."

# 16

# TIME TO CELEBRATE

The posters stuck to walls across Riobamba. A caricatured Indian peasant looked out at passersby, and beneath him the bold lettering declared: "For the Liberty of the Oppressed, Summer Institute of Linguistics Get Out of Here!"

Organizers had plastered the signs all over town in preparation for a rally against the Wycliffe Bible Translators-related Summer Institute of Linguistics (SIL). However, the political and religious activists also targeted practically every other evangelical agency in Ecuador in their demand, "Get out of here!"

Seeing the posters, Quichua church leader Basilio Malán knew the bewildered Indian on the poster was supposed to represent the Quichuas in Chimborazo. But it certainly did not represent *him*.

"I don't feel oppressed," thought Malán, president of the Indigenous Evangelical Association of Chimborazo. "I feel free."

The missionaries had never done anything to hurt him, Basilio thought. As a boy in Pulucate, he had carried water for the single women missionaries. They had taught him to read and write, and they had told him about Jesus. He was baptized in that first Quichua baptism in 1955. If it had not been for the missionaries, he might never have heard the gospel.

Even more than the attack against missionaries, some-

115

thing bothered Basilio. "If these people are allowed to drive out the missionaries, they might go after all of us Quichua evangelicals next," he commented in the home of missionary Roberta Hostetter.

Basilio was not about to forget those years of persecution as a new Christian. At first, he and his uncle had not been faithful in their Christian walk. Before visiting the missionaries, the uncle would sometimes have to tell Basilio, "Let's brush our teeth so they won't know we've been drinking."

As a young married man, Basilio decided one day to observe a nearby fiesta. He did not expect to drink—only watch the dancing. Basilio picked up his poncho and whip and started out the house.

Basilio's wife, Mercedes, knew where her husband was going. She said, "Listen. How is it the Bible says, 'No man can serve two masters?'"

Mercedes came from the Naula family in El Troje, the village where Quichua believers first stood firm amid persecution. "In El Troje," she said, "we don't attend the fiestas." She said nothing else and got up to fetch water.

Basilio walked slowly away and climbed to the top of a high hill and sat down. Mercedes's words pounded in his head. "No man can serve two masters."

Basilio did not go to the feast that day. And he never went back to drink or lukewarm Christianity. He stood firm, even when feast-goers dumped liquor on his head. He considered Mercedes the person who most influenced his Christian life.

Now in 1981, some people still wanted to stop the evangelicals, but their methods were more subtle.

It used to be that people put the Quichuas down with the expressed intention of hurting them. Now, they were subduing the Quichuas under the guise of helping them.

"The evangelicals are destroying the Indians' culture," intellectuals said in their attacks on the missionaries.

"But that's foolish," Basilio told Roberta. "We have kept our typical music, our customs and our language." Nearly 450 years of Spanish rule had not eliminated Quichua culture, so how could the critics assume the missionaries had

116

done that in only a few years?

No, the missionaries had not changed the Quichuas' culture, Basilio felt. *God* had changed the Quichuas, on the inside, in their hearts. As a result, many negative aspects of their culture had withered away.

Less than twenty years earlier, drunken Quichuas filled the mestizos' saloons and littered the highways. How many thousands of Quichua fathers used to wake up with their heads pounding and their money spent or stolen? What Quichua man, in his rage and drunkenness, had not beaten his wife and children only to hate himself for it later? How many Quichuas had gotten cut and bruised in the wild brawls?

Now that Quichua Christians were not spending all of their money on *chicha*, they provided better for their families. Believers were able to afford cement-block homes, rather than the mud-walled ones.

Seeing these changes, onlookers mistakenly scoffed, "Oh, you people become evangelicals so you can get rich."

Basilio remembered the inauguration ceremony for a new school in San Antonio. An official from the Ministry of Education reminded his Quichua listeners—nearly all of them evangelicals—of how they previously had lived in mud huts and traveled dirt roads.

"Now, look at you," he said. "You have good houses and good roads. You've got better food and health than you ever had before. Just look what education has done for you."

An elderly man could not contain himself. "Education nothing," he objected. "It's the gospel that did this. The gospel came in here and transformed our lives."

As Basilio and Roberta conversed, he happened to spot a copy of the book *Along the Quichua Trail* by Ben Nickel, which described the early history of the Quichua church in Chimborazo. But Basilio's mind was on other things as he listlessly leafed from page to page.

As president of the Quichua evangelical association, he felt responsible for his fellow Quichua believers. Quichuas liked parades, so Basilio hoped the evangelicals would not

117

take part in the protest rally, ignorant of the real nature of the event.

Slowly an idea started forming in his mind. What if the evangelical association organized something positive at the same time as the protest rally? It could be like when the missionaries organized church conferences as a Christian alternative to Carnival and the fiestas.

Why couldn't the evangelicals show the critics they *were* proud of being Quichuas? Why couldn't they proclaim the great things Christianity had done for them?

Looking down at the book, Basilio's eyes fell on a picture of the founding of the Quichua Christian radio station. He had been one of the first announcers, and he had gone into remote villages with a tape recorder to get interviews for programs. Basilio read very little English, but he noticed the station's inauguration date: December 5, 1961. That was almost exactly twenty years ago!

"We can celebrate this!" he exclaimed, hurriedly running out of the house.

### Radio's 20th anniversary

Basilio called a meeting of the AIECH leaders, and he shared his idea of celebrating the twentieth anniversary of the radio station, which GMU had turned over to the Association in 1975. Basilio proposed they hold the celebration the same weekend as the Riobamba protest rally, December 12.

"But there are only ten days until the rally," someone said.

"Then we'll just have to work fast," Basilio replied.

The machinery of the Indigenous Evangelical Association of Chimborazo started rolling. A mammoth vehicle of evangelical humanity, the association had formed in 1966 when there were only 300 Quichua evangelicals. Now the Association had 7,600 individual members—all baptized dues-paying believers in good standing in one of the province's 200 Quichua evangelical churches.

The Association's many departments included a savings

118

and loan. No longer did the Quichua evangelicals have to make the long trip to Riobamba only to be told they did not qualify for a loan. The Association had also formed a transportation cooperative, *Nuca Llacta*, with its fleet of buses painted red, yellow and blue—the colors of Ecuador's flag. The buses took Quichuas up the winding mountain trails to remote villages, whereas the local buses only went down the main highways. And as part of its evangelistic program, the Association also bought some bright orange tents, manufactured in Texas, which between them held several thousand people at the popular church conferences.

The Association had so much activity Basilio could hardly keep on top of things. The other Quichua church leaders were busy, too. So how could the Association put together an anniversary celebration for the radio station in less than two weeks?

## Promoting the celebration

Basilio and the others threw themselves into organizing and promoting the event. They advertised by radio and word of mouth. Invitations went to Quichua evangelicals in other Ecuadorian provinces, as well as to government officials. Basilio even invited Archbishop Proaño of Riobamba, who was involved in the effort to oust the Summer Institute of Linguistics, and known opponents of the evangelical movement, who all declined.

To celebrate Quichua culture, organizers asked attenders to wear their typical clothing and bring their traditional food. A parade, styled after the old fiesta celebrations, was also planned.

The full weekend program called for soccer championships, Christian music contests and the election of new officers for the Association.

Anticipation mounted the day before the three-day celebration. Men hooked together two of the large fluorescent orange tents. They made cushiony tent floors out of freshly-cut grass from the páramo, the high-altitude plateau above the tree line.

119

Now all that remained was the waiting. Would the evangelicals come? Had there been enough time for people to find out about the celebration?

On Friday, December 11, the first day of the celebration, Quichua families started arriving in trucks, buses and cars. Others walked. By Saturday, so many people had come that the Association wondered whether the field below the old mission station could hold everyone.

Manuel Naula Sagñay, the Quichuas' first medical doctor and a former teacher at the boarding school, asked, "How are we ever going to feed them all?"

Fortunately, a horde of enterprising food vendors stood ready with their big iron pots of soup and potatoes. Roasted *cuy*, guinea pigs, sent up a tantalizing aroma for Quichua attenders. In addition, volunteers cooked food and sold it as a money-making project for the Association.

On Saturday morning the Association sent people into Riobamba to buy more food. In Riobamba one of the buyers witnessed the anti-missionary rally, now underway. He estimated the turnout at barely 3,000—most of them not Quichuas. He thought the marchers looked somber, even frightened.

Meanwhile back in Colta, attendance figures varied between 10,000 and 30,000. By everyone's estimation, this was the largest public gathering of Chimborazo Quichuas in history.

Missionary Phyllis Blum parked her car among the people, and from it she sold Quichua Bibles and literature.

"Where's Phyllis?" co-workers asked, when she did not come back for lunch.

"I didn't leave, because I was afraid that I would never be able to get back to the car in all those people," she explained afterwards.

### A truly Quichua event

During the weekend, evangelicals did everything that was traditionally "Quichua," except for the drinking. During tent meetings at night, some forty ordained Quichua pastors took turns preaching. Delighted attenders sang the original Quichua hymns into the wee hours of the morning.

In a festive crowd of that size—kind of like a Quichua evangelical Woodstock—the missionaries feared injuries. But not one accident was reported. On the contrary, observers and outsiders frequently complimented the Quichuas on their peaceful and orderly conduct.

By the time the celebration ended, the Quichua believers had given an impressive visible account of themselves. If nothing else, they demonstrated the strength of their churches. With at least 10,000 baptized Quichua evangelicals in Chimborazo Province, and an overall worshiping community approaching 40,000, the evangelicals formed a good chunk of the population.

After it was all over, Basilio Malán commented to a missionary, "I guess maybe this proves we Quichua evangelicals aren't going to sit by while people try to get rid of the missionaries."

"It's proven something else to me," said the missionary, thinking of how the Quichuas had planned, paid for and promoted the celebration all by the themselves.

"Even if the missionaries had to leave today, the Quichua church would go on."

**17**

# THE GOSPEL IS FOR YOU, TOO

Henry Klassen was splitting wood outside his house when I walked up the lane toward the old Gospel Missionary Union compound in Majipamba, Chimborazo Province. Henry took a break and stretched out his hand.

He sat down on a pile of logs as big around as a man's waist. "I planted those trees more than thirty years ago when we came to Colta," Klassen said.

Beside us a few yards away was the "cemetery," the grassy fenced-in plot that Quichua evangelicals used during the 1950s when they were denied burial in local cemeteries. Nearly 100 people were buried there—"all but a few of them children."

Klassen was wearing his characteristic Western string tie. He still chuckles about the time a Riobamba shopkeeper asked about the tie, "Is that part of your religion?" Another woman once asked Klassen to order her two of the ties which she wanted to use with a new dress.

This was my sixth trip to Chimborazo: I wanted one last update—from missionaries and Quichuas alike—before wrapping up this book. Also, where was the church heading?

Klassen, who had worked among the Quichuas since 1953 and before I was born, probably knew the situation better than any non-Quichua. After Pat Klassen prepared breakfast again—this time for the visitor—we discussed the current status of the Quichua church from the missionary's point of view.

The latest 1988 figures showed 329 Quichua evangelical churches in the Chimborazo Province, Klassen said. These were churches identifying with the Association of Indigenous Evangelical Churches of Chimborazo (AIECH) and the original work begun by Gospel Missionary Union. Chimborazo believers had started churches in other areas of Ecuador and other countries of South America, but "as their home base they usually name Chimborazo."

A few different church groups had started work in Chimborazo, including a "slain in the Spirit" Pentecostal group and a "prosperity gospel" group from the US, said Klassen. But the vast majority of Quichua evangelical groups in Chimborazo belonged to the Association, *La Union*, said Klassen.

As to membership, "the Mission feels there are about 30,000 Quichua believers," Klassen said. "The Quichuas put it at 50,000."

When the Klassens first went to Chimborazo, they hoped to start at least one Quichua congregation. The subsequent growth far exceeded their expectations. Asked by a journalist to explain the growth, Klassen had said, "Technically, if you want an answer, it would be the homogeneous unit principle.

"Before, we tried to put the Quichuas in with our Spanish work. We'd take the Quichuas to the Spanish church conventions. After awhile, the Quichuas said they didn't want to go anymore. They were tired of being guinea pigs with everyone looking at them funny."

### Recent developments

As to recent developments, Klassen noted the recent founding of a small seminary in Colta, then in its second year with nine students.

I had arrived in Chimborazo on the heels of a big evangelism congress, planned and mostly paid for by the Quichua churches as follow up to Billy Graham's 1986 Amsterdam conference. For a "feast-oriented people" like the Quichuas, the conference was "important and a real encouragement," said Klassen. Pastors were following up the nearly 1,000 attenders who made first-time commitments or rededicated their lives to Christ.

Continuing a tradition begun in the early 1950s, the missionaries still conducted Bible institutes. About 100 students were involved in the four-year program. A year's studies are divided into three two-week segments, held in Colta.

Missions interest is slow, but coming, said Klassen. There are a few pockets of Quichuas unreached by the gospel in Chimborazo, "but the Quichuas are involved in reaching them...it's harder for the missionary to go into those unreached areas and evangelize."

Today the missionaries teach and preach only when they are invited by the Quichua churches. "One of the hardest things about letting go, is that you don't always know what's going on [in the churches]," Pat Klassen said.

Are more North American missionaries still needed? "Yes, but only if they are teaching missionaries, who can identify with the Quichuas," said Klassen.

One of the biggest problems in the Quichua church is money, Klassen said. Since GMU does not financially support Quichua pastors or build church buildings, some Quichua leaders today "are finding it is easier just to go to Quito and ask the missions for money," Klassen said.

(The director of an evangelical relief and development agency in Quito confessed that different agencies "have turned the Chimborazo Quichuas into professional beggars, looking for what they can get," and he said efforts were being made to correct the problem.)

Among other challenges and needs facing Quichua evangelicals, Klassen listed: marriage and family problems, the need for more Quichua theologians, Bible study materials for the laity, and "a lot of good teaching on the basics."

Quichua and Spanish evangelicals still distrust one another, Klassen said. When Spanish church leaders asked the Quichuas for statistics in preparation for the 1987 Latin

American missions congress, COMIBAM, in Sao Paulo, Brazil, the Quichuas would not give them any information. Also, there remains the tendency among some Quichuas to "accept Christ in their culture but not in their heart."

Our talk about church problems reminded Klassen of some short-term missionaries who visited the Quichua work. One young man said, "I'm sure glad I came, because now I've seen there are some negatives in missions. Why don't you missionaries tell us about the negatives?"

"Look at it this way," Klassen responded. "You go back to a North America church after seven or eight years, and the pastor gives you five or ten minutes to speak. Now you tell me—will you talk about the negatives or the positives?"

"Well, I'd probably talk about the positives."

"You see," said Klassen. "That's one reason why we like people to come down here—so they can see some of the negatives."

## Time for a movie

Late Sunday afternoon, a young man, Hilario, showed up at the Klassen house. He was from San Antonio de Chaupi, a village about thirty minutes away where Klassen had promised to show a Christian film that night.

As he had done countless times before, Klassen loaded his generator and film projector into his fourteen-year-old Land Rover with more than 100,000 miles on it. We headed south down the Pan American Highway. Hilario indicated the turn-off, and we bounced through chuckholes and along the edges of ravines as we climbed a narrow road to the village.

Like most Quichua young people today, Hilario spoke Spanish as well as Quichua. He said the road was put in only four years ago, and officials had promised to come with tractors and widen it. Before the road, the people going to market had carried everything out on their backs.

The village was even getting running water: a community faucet had been installed. Tall concrete poles, sticking like tall gray toothpicks on the surrounding mountainsides, bore witness that San Antonio de Chaupi would also have electricity. Like so many other Quichua evangelical churches, "Light of the World" sat on the highest hilltop in the community. It was getting dark when we arrived, and the church windows flickered orange from five lit candles inside.

"*Alabado*," said a tiny boy, seeing me, a white-skinned *gringo*. A Quichua man laughed. "That's how Quichuas used to salute the white man," he told me. The phrase loosely means, "May you be praised."

The meeting started with singing lasting at least an hour. Meanwhile, the worship leader promoted the soon-to-be-shown film through a loudspeaker he had rigged up in the window. Somehow in the black night, men, women and children found their way up the winding narrow path to the church.

Before the movie, Henry signaled me to follow him into a small room off the side of the church. There some women sat on their haunches stirring big black kettles. We were motioned to sit on a small bench, and a man brought us soup. It had potatoes and the Quichua delicacy, guinea pig.

In keeping with Quichua hospitality, we were served a second bowl. The soup tasted good in the cold Andean air. But we could not finish all the food, so Henry, the experienced one, spooned our leftovers into a plastic "doggie" bag so as not to offend our generous hosts.

After finishing, we shook hands with everyone in the room, according to Quichua custom. Once a North American visitor complained to Henry, "Don't they ever get tired of shaking hands?"

We returned with the enthusiastic singing still in progress. It used to be that Quichua Christians didn't use the guitar, Henry said, because believers associated it with the fiestas. Churches didn't use the drum either until the members of a well-known band converted. Since that time people joked, "We've converted the drum," Klassen said.

Films always seem to draw crowds, and the church was

jammed when the movie began. Henry simultaneously translated into Quichua the entire hour-long Cathedral Films release about Jesus's crucifixion. The viewers hissed between their teeth at scenes that particularly impressed them.

It was getting close to midnight when we left. Stars spattered across a cold clear sky. Meanwhile, the service was finishing. About 75 percent of the attenders were children. Hilario had said the Quichua churches' biggest challenge was ministering to young people. I couldn't help but wonder what would happen to these youngsters and their church in their changing world of running water, roads and electric lights.

**Visit to the radio station**

Early the next morning, I walked across Majipamba from the Klassens' house to the Quichua radio station, the "Radio Voice of the Indigenous Association of Chimborazo."

Station manager Jorge Viñan emphasized radio's importance in maintaining communication between Quichua believers in the outlying communities.

Before his conversion in 1971, Viñan worked for the Catholic radio station *Radiofónicas* in Riobamba. He could never understand why the priests criticized the evangelicals, so he investigated.

"Why is it bad to be an evangelical?" he asked then Archbishop of Riobamba, Leonidas Proaño.

"It's not bad to be an evangelical," Proaño said, somewhat to Viñan's surprise. "What's bad is being mediocre."

Viñan kept investigating the evangelicals, and the more he saw, the more he liked. So he asked another priest why he opposed the evangelicals. "They are servants of the Yankees," the man said.

Viñan returned once more to Proaño and again asked, "Why is it bad to be an evangelical?"

"It's not bad," Proaño said.

"Then I'm going to accept the Lord," Viñan said. Shortly afterward, he made a public profession of faith at a campaign in San Bernardo under Agustín Añilema. Jorge continued working for *Radiofónicas* another ten years.

Noting former Archbishop Proaño's nomination for the Nobel Peace Prize, Viñan said, "Many people say that he evangelized. But we don't believe he was the one. Here in Chimborazo, the Bible entered through other persons, not through him. The evangelization occurred through other persons, the missionaries, not through him.

"And the change that took place in the Quichuas of Chimborazo was not because Proaño said something. It was the product of the gospel."

### "St. Peter—Can you hear me?"

Interestingly, another Quichua church leader found his faith indirectly through the influence of a Roman Catholic priest. Nicolás Guambo, president in 1987 and 1988 of the Quichua association AIECH, was a Roman Catholic catechist as a young man in his village of Puesitús.

As a young man, Guambo had questioned the Quichuas' reverence of idols and images of the saints. Every time he taught the Ten Commandments, he felt guilty when he taught about not worshiping graven images.

After a series of disillusioning experiences in the church, Guambo attended a feast for Saint Peter that a friend was sponsoring. Guambo was drunk when he joined the religious procession going toward the church for mass.

Musicians, community leaders and male and female feast-goers filled the church building, and the priest—a young cleric new to the area—looked sternly at all of them.

"What feast are you observing?" he asked.

"*Padrecito*, we're celebrating the feast of *San Pedro*," said the village leader.

"Where's Saint Peter?" the priest demanded.

"Don't you see? He's over there, sitting down," the village leader said, pointing to a small statue of the saint.

The priest looked severely at the Quichua parishioners.

"Listen," he said. "We're going to do a test. If Saint Peter answers me, I'm going to conduct the mass. If he doesn't, I'm not going to lead the mass. I'm going to call him three times. If he answers me, I also am going to worship Saint Peter."

Hearing this, Guambo felt his earlier doubts being confirmed. "Honored commissary, ladies and gentlemen," the priest began. "Saint Peter! Do you hear?"

There was no response. "Now I'm going to call a second time. Saint Peter! Can you hear?"

Again there was nothing. After he yelled "Saint Peter" a third time with the same result, the priest walked out.

After this experience, "I didn't have the heart to stay in the area," Guambo said. He went to Guayaquil, threw away his religious relics and professed faith in Christ at an evangelical church. He noticed that a chronic pain in his back disappeared after his prayer for conversion.

The pastor asked Guambo if there were other believers in his community. When Guambo said no, the pastor surprised him by starting to weep. He laid his hands on Guambo, and prayed, "God, protect this man. There is no one to protect him. Only you."

Guambo returned to his community at fiesta time and began to testify to his new faith. People began to beat him, and they forced him to drink. Guambo returned to the Guayaquil pastor and asked for help. After four months of solid Bible teaching, Guambo again returned to his community and this time, "there was no one who could stop me. I began to preach whether people wanted me to or not. And people converted."

Religious fanatics and community leaders tried to beat and lynch Guambo. They even hired a witch doctor to cast a deadly spell on Guambo. The witch doctor said the job would cost lots of money and take at least six months. "No!" the persecutors complained. "In six months, he'll start six more churches." Guambo, meanwhile, kept right on preaching. He became a pastor in 1966.

Early in 1988, a fanatical mob in the isolated Chimborazo village of Totoras did lynch a Quichua evangelist, Antonio Zuma. Guambo said the Quichua Association immediately investigated the murder—even getting help from some Catholic authorities—and they came up with the names of eight persons believed to have been involved. The Association spent more than 300,000 Ecuadorian sucres in its legal battle for justice in the matter. One suspect was captured. Then the church association organized a march of 2,000 people into the community where the killing had taken place. The rest of the suspects got scared, said Guambo. "They thought we were going to do something to them, and they surrendered...the Lord did it all."

Guambo, a thickset man with a Dick Butkus build, said maybe the Quichua churches need a little of the old persecution to get back their evangelistic fire and fervor of earlier days.

### "It almost makes me weep"

Klassen took me to visit his old friend, Matías Mullo, the gentle "patriarch" from El Troje. Matías was concerned about the Quichua youth.

"Now that we are Christians, we live better, we have better houses, and we have more income. But I'm concerned for our young people, who are striving more for materialism than God's work, more for the material than the spiritual."

He remembers the times of suffering and persecution, and still doesn't know all the reasons for it. "But there have been so many happy days," he said. "It almost makes me weep when I think of how the Lord has protected me, and how he's changed my life."

I also talked with Basilio Malán, working for World Vision in Riobamba. He talked about his growing up years in Pulucate, when fathers neglected their wives and children and were only concerned about "drinking and more drinking—we didn't even have clothes. The little that we harvested, they sold. Maybe at harvest time we had a little barley to eat.

"But thanks to God, we Christians are now concerned about giving our children an education. Before, the Quichua women were treated as if they were worthless. The woman had to wash and grind grain, nothing more. "To be an example for other believers, I put my daughters in school. And now, everyone has their daughters in school. I've told my children about the suffering. I don't say we have such a good life, but we have at least enough to eat and educate our children. This has meant a big, big difference for the Quichua people."

He alluded to the Quichuas' new sense of worth and value as people. I was reminded that many observers point to a Quichua "Indian rights" movement as part of the reason for church growth.

Luis Asitimbay, who called himself "the primary persecutor" of the evangelicals in San Antonio before his conversion, had recently been elected *teniente político*, the political leader, in his village, now called Santiago de Quito.

In 1984 some friends took his truck into an outlying community to evangelize, and a drunken mob destroyed the vehicle. Luis returned there to preach early in 1988, and more than 125 people accepted the Lord as personal Savior.

**Need for leaders**

I visited nearly four hours with pioneer church leader in Colta, Manuel Bahua Cajas. He described the growth of the Quichua church, as well as his active role in preaching and evangelism. "I'm thankful for all that God has done." But Bahua said that he was not actively involved in the local church.

For various reasons, other early leaders in the Quichua church had departed from the local church scene. One left the public ministry due to marital problems. Another left to work with a different denomination in Quito. Other former pastors went to work for evangelical organizations that could pay them a salary. One of the original church leaders in Colta shocked everyone when he suddenly joined the Jehovah's Witnesses. And certain others had been removed from their ministries for different indiscretions.

One leader who does remain firm is José Manuel Naula,

son of Juan Naula who opened his home to the missionaries in El Troje. When I interviewed him, José Manuel was directing Quichua programming for World Radio HCJB in Quito and pastoring a Quichua congregation in the city.

"Perhaps I don't always defend the missionaries," said the gifted preacher and evangelist. "But I must say thank-you and express my gratitude to them for opening our minds, for opening our spiritual eyes, so that we ourselves could seek God. We ourselves now have Jesus Christ."

He believes he is located in a strategic spot, since more and more Quichua evangelicals are moving to the capital city to get a better education, said Naula.

"The [political] extremists say the evangelicals are abandoning the countryside and that they don't want to work," said Naula. "But that's a lie. Quichuas come to attend university, to get schooling, because they can't get it in the country. They want to get ahead."

The eight or so Quichua churches in Quito "have the opportunity to train these people here so they can return to their communities and be defenders of the gospel," said Naula.

He responded to the criticism that evangelicals damage the Quichua culture.

"When I was a boy, my parents didn't change clothes or perhaps even bathe for three weeks or a month. Our culture was that way. We didn't cut or wash our hair either. I remember—and I'm not exaggerating—when I had head lice as a boy. The only thing I did was tend sheep in the fields. Nothing more.

"My parents spent their time in the feasts. They weren't concerned about us. And that's how we lived. But now, I have a son. He's not like I was at his age. Since he was small, he's had shoes. He's had clean clothes. We have changed, but for our own good. This is the kind of change the gospel made—for our own good. My children have changed, but for their own good."

Like many of the other Quichua leaders I interviewed, José Manuel was especially concerned about the future vitality of the Quichua church. At the Billy Grahamsponsored Amsterdam congress in 1986, "in very few churches did I see the love of God. There are many things there—money, jobs. And the people seem to live happily, but not all have the love of God.

"I thought afterwards. What will happen to us, the Quichua evangelicals? If we don't do something, we may end up the same way."

## "God has been at work"

Interviews finished, I took a multitude of thoughts aboard the airplane from Quito to Guayaquil, en route to Miami. It was remarkable how much liquor the passengers managed to consume in a thirty-minute flight. This was some flying fiesta. I was seeing more booze here than during all my time in Chimborazo.

It would seem that roles have reversed and today an increasing number of Quichuas are the good example, not the bad one.

During the early years of the Quichua revival, Henry Klassen had gone to Quito for a visit. After church one Sunday night, he went out for coffee at one of the local hotels. There in the restaurant he spotted one of his neighbors from Colta, a Spanish landowner named Chávez, drinking with some friends.

*Señor* Chávez saw Klassen and quickly got up from his table. He came over and gave the surprised missionary a big Latin bear hug.

"I'm so glad to see you," he told Klassen. "I've got something to tell you."

Chávez was not normally this warm and effusive. Klassen could tell the man was just enough under the influence of alcohol not to care what he said or with whom he spoke publicly.

"What is it you want to tell me?" asked Klassen, curious.

"You know, one of my Quichua foremen on the hacienda has become an evangelical," Chávez began. "He is so different now, and I can't figure him out. Before he would steal from me, and I only kept him on because he was a good worker.

"Just last week, we were down there bagging potatoes. And this fellow came up to me and said, 'Look, *amito*, boss, here's a needle somebody dropped. I found it while we were cleaning up.'

'What on earth has happened to you, Manuel? You used to steal me blind. Now you find a needle and give it to me. Is that what your religion does to you?'

"Well, yes, I'm an evangelical. I'm honest. I don't steal and I don't lie. I want to live in a way that pleases God," the Quichua convert said.

The landowner looked him up and down. "Well, if that's what your religion does to you. Go ahead and do it."

"Then you know what Manuel told me?" the landowner said incredulously to Klassen. "'*Amito*, this gospel isn't just for me. It's for you too.'"

The landowner hesitated, looking over at the table where his drinking buddies still sat, and he confessed, "I can't leave my friends and go to another religion. Manuel is a better man than I am."

Remembering this encounter, Klassen told me, "Oh, there is such a change from what the Quichuas were to what they are now...and there's still room for change."

Of the Quichuas' evangelical people movement, Klassen could only say, "How can you explain all this? God has been at work. It wasn't any particular method or program. We have just been God's instruments."

I left Ecuador, amazed once again by the transformation of the Quichuas and convinced that God will carry forward and complete his work among them.

# 18

# SHE KNEW GOD

Julia Anderson Woodward: the missionary who spent nearly half a century among Ecuador's Quichuas and never saw more than a handful of converts.

That is how Mrs. Woodward is usually remembered, and we tend to pity her. How could anyone work so long with so few visible results?

However, former colleagues of Mrs. Woodward indicated the last thing Mrs. Woodward would have wanted was pity. In interviews, they painted a compelling, often surprising, portrait of this pioneer missionary.

I asked them what kept Mrs. Woodward going during all those years with so few visible results. What kind of a person was she?

"Only a person of courage and dedication and one who had felt the call of God to such a ministry would or could have endured the opposition that she endured," said Leona Brownlee Malic, who served with Mrs. Woodward in Caliata during the late 1940s and 1950s.

"When the work becomes more difficult, pray more," said a note Mrs. Malic later found in Julia Woodward's Bible.

Former co-workers marveled at her self-discipline and the way she put God first. They remembered her flashes of humor, her appreciation for poetry and beauty and the way she acted just as comfortably in the fine homes of American diplomats and businessmen as she did in dirt-floored Quichua huts.

Friends said she was firm, but not rigid; a hard worker but not a workaholic; a strict teacher, but a patient one.

In the latter part of her missionary career, Mrs. Woodward often taught or lived with the younger, single female missionaries. One of them, Mrs. Pauline Tallman, rather feared her first encounter with Julia Woodward—some of the other missionaries had said she was "bossy."

Expecting to meet a "tyrant in army boots," the new missionary was in for a pleasant surprise. "I liked her immediately. She was tall and slender—stately—with grace and warmth."

Soon after her arrival in Ecuador, Pauline said, "I wanted to play an April Fool's trick on her, but I hesitated. I wasn't sure she would appreciate something so frivolous at her expense.

"When she commented on the rain falling, and I realized we were under sunny skies, I knew who the fool was in our house."

During her first year on the mission field in 1940, Jean Mann Johnson lived with Mrs. Woodward in Caliata. The work was discouraging, but the new missionary observed "the Quichuas always respected Mrs. Woodward. They would come to her with their problems, and urge her to visit their homes."

Mrs. Woodward rarely if ever talked about past tragedies in her life, and she did not complain about the hardships of mountain life, said Johnson. But if one of the newer workers lamented the hardships of mountain life, Mrs. Woodward did not especially appreciate it.

When Jean complained one day about the cold in Caliata, Woodward said, "Aren't you sensible enough to wear cotton stockings?"

The two women had met young single missionary Ernest Johnson in Guayaquil. He was in poor health from working in the jungle. "What you need is some mountain air," said Woodward, inviting him up to Chimborazo to fix a leaking roof. During his six weeks in Caliata, a romance developed between him and Jean.

The couple eventually married, and "I would kid Julia that it was her fault that I didn't stay in Quichua work," said Mrs. Johnson.

Former co-worker Margaret McGivney remembered Mrs. Woodward's "singleness of heart and faithfulness to the Lord." She said Mrs. Woodward tried to take care of her health—otherwise she would have never lived so long under such difficult conditions.

"She had a personal dignity that protected her in her younger years from many dangers," said McGivney. "She told me her closest call came while riding her horse in a lonely area. A man stopped her, taking hold of the horse's bridle. She raised her whip and hit him with all her might and galloped away before he could recover."

McGivney remembered two of Julia Woodward's "life verses," which the missionary often quoted: I Samuel 2:30—"Them that honor me, I will honor"; and Proverbs 4:23—"Keep thy heart with all diligence; for out of it are the issues of life."

Another missionary remembered, "She was so humble. She acted as if she had never suffered."

Doing translation work into her late sixties, Mrs. Woodward relaxed from mental exhaustion by reading or writing poetry—her lifelong hobby. Occasionally the missionary crocheted or did jigsaw puzzles. Somewhere she had gotten a Chinese Checkers game, and to relax she would play all sides of the board against herself. "She said it cleared her mind," said a co-worker.

Never in especially good health, Mrs. Woodward pressed on to finish her Quichua New Testament translation, a lasting and major contribution to the Quichua revival that followed.

Mrs. Woodward did live to hear about the first Quichua baptisms in Ecuador's Chimborazo Province and construction of the first churches. But the big spiritual breakthrough came after her death in 1960 at age eighty-three in a Kansas City nursing home.

Yet somehow, the issue doesn't seem to be whether Mrs. Woodward led 10, 50 or 1,000 Quichuas to the Lord. Most important, she was faithful to the work to which she believed God had called her. In contrast to this day of short-term missionary service and frenetic career changes, Mrs. Woodward gave more than fifty years of her life in Christian service to one country and one people.

"Perhaps the most outstanding thing about Mrs. Woodward was that she knew herself and she knew God," recalled Jean Mann Johnson.

"She knew her own frailties....She knew her lack of education did not make her the ideal one to translate Scriptures. But she knew God had called her and was able to use a yielded vessel. Opposition, tragedies, failures, lack of perfect health and wide acceptance—none of these moved her to give up doing what she knew God wanted her to do.

"I am sure the Lord will reward her for her faithfulness, and I believe he used her to challenge many others to prayer and/or service to the Quichuas."

Back in 1903, decades before the Quichua spiritual revival, Julia Anderson Woodward had said, "At times I think of the future, and I fancy that I can see souls saved and hear Indians singing the Gospel."

Now, as part of that "cloud of witnesses" mentioned in Scripture, Julia Woodward is hearing those hymns, most of which were written by the Quichuas themselves. Today there is *a new song in the Andes*. Today, thousands of Quichuas have the music of Jesus, their Savior, in their hearts. Thank God Julia Woodward, fellow missionaries, and those first Quichua believers never gave up. Thank God for a people transformed on the slopes of the Andes.

# CHRONOLOGY

| | |
|---|---|
| 1896 | Liberal government of General Eloy Alfaro permits Protestant missionaries into Ecuador. |
| 1902 | Julia Anderson and Ella Ozman move to Ecuador's Chimborazo Province and begin ministry to the Quichuas in the village of Caliata. |
| 1903 | Ozman dies of pneumonia, and Anderson continues alone. |
| 1915-1928 | Quichua work is sporadic following Anderson's marriage to fellow Gospel Missionary Union (GMU) worker William Woodward. Woodward dies in 1926, and Julia returns to full-time ministry in Chimborazo. |
| 1950 | GMU opens a second mission station for Quichua work in Pulucate. |
| 1953 | Julia Anderson Woodward retires from missionary service. GMU purchases the mission station in Colta, and missionaries Henry and Pat Klassen move there. |
| 1954 | The Quichua New Testament is published and arrives for distribution in Chimborazo. |
| 1955 | The first three Quichua believers are baptized in Lake Colta. |
| 1958 | The first Quichua church is built in El Troje. |

| | |
|---|---|
| 1961 | Quichua Christian radio station HCUE-5 is inaugurated in Colta. |
| 1964 | Ecuadorian government approves land reform legislation. |
| 1965 | Twenty-two Quichua families in San Antonio, who become Christians in three weeks' time, withstand heavy persecution. |
| 1966 | Quichua believers form an association, the Indigenous Evangelical Association of Chimborazo (AIECH). |
| 1971 | Three Quichuas ordained as lay pastors. Some 155 believers are baptized in one service at San Bernardo. GMU's Atahualpa School is turned over to the community. |
| 1973 | New translation of Quichua New Testament is presented with more than 5,000 in attendance. |
| 1975 | The Colta-based radio station is turned over to the Quichua association. |
| 1981 | The Quichua radio's twentieth anniversary celebration draws more than 10,000 people to Colta. |
| 1988 | Old Testament translation complete, the complete Bible in Chimborazo Quichua is scheduled for publication by the United Bible Societies. Estimates of total baptized Quichua evangelical in Chimborazo range from 30,000 to 50,000. |

| | |
|---|---|
| 1988 | More than 30,000 attend "Hermano Pablo" evangelistic campaign. Nearly 1,000 decisions for salvation or recommitment. |
| 1990 | Evangelistic campaign with Albeto Motesse Team. |
| 1991 | Churches and congregations—335<br>Belivers—78,500<br>Christian constituency—100,180 |

# FOR FURTHER READING

Brown, Roger H.
1977    *Kingdom of the Sun*. Bath, England: Echoes of
        Service.

Dilworth, Donald R.
1967    "The Evangelization of the Quichuas of Ecuador."
        An unpublished M.A. thesis submitted at the Fuller
        School of World Mission, Fuller Theological
        Seminary, in Pasadena, CA.

Klassen, Jacob Peter.
1974    "Fire on the Páramo: A New Day in Quichua
        Receptivity." An unpublished M.A. thesis submitted
        at the Fuller School of World Mission, Fuller
        Theological Seminary, in Pasadena, CA.

Maynard, Eileen.
1966    *The Indians of Colta: Essays on the Colta Lake
        Zone, Chimborazo (Ecuador)*. Ithaca, NY:
        Department of Anthropology, Cornell University.

McIntyre, Loren.
1975    *The Incredible Incas and Their Timeless Land*.
        Washington, D.C.: National Geographic Society.

Muratorio, Blanca.
1981    "Protestantism, Ethnicity and Class in Chimbo-
        razo," pp. 506-534, in *Cultural Transformations
        and Ethnicity in Modern Ecuador*, Norman E.
        Whitten, Jr. ed. Urbana: University of Illinois Press.

Nickel, Ben J.
1965    *Along the Quichua Trail*. Smithville, MO: Gospel
        Missionary Union.

Padilla, Washington.
1987 "El Protestantismo en el Ecuador: Breve Reseña
Historica," Boletín Teologico. Fraternidad Teo-
lógica Latinoamericana: Buenos Aires, Argentina.

Paredes Alfaro, Ruben Eli.
1980 "A Protestant Movement in Ecuador and Peru: A
Comparative Socio-Anthropological Study of the
Establishment and Diffusion of Protestantism in
Two Central Highland Regions," doctoral disserta-
tion, Los Angeles: University of California.

Von Hagen, Victor Wolfgang, ed.
1959 The Incas of Pedro de Cieza de Leon. Harriet de
Onis, translator. Norman, Oklahoma: University of
Oklahoma Press.